Big Ole PIECE OF Cake

by **Sean McLoughlin**

Fishamble: The New Play Company is funded by the
Arts Council/An Chomhairle Ealaíon.
It is also supported by Dublin City Council and its international
touring is supported by Culture Ireland.

Fishamble: The New Play Company

Fishamble: The New Play Company wishes to thank the following following Friends of Fishamble for their invaluable support:

Big Dreamers
Helen Cunningham
Andrew & Delyth Parkes
Vincent O'Doherty

Trailblazers
Robert & Lilian Chambers
Brian Friel

Movers & Shakers
Dearbhail Ann Shannon
David & Veronica Rowe
Alan & Caroline Gray

Thank you also to those who do not wish to be credited.

For further details on how to become a Friend of Fishamble please see
www.fishamble.com **or contact** info@fishamble.com

Fishamble wishes to thank the following for their support with
Big Ole Piece of Cake:
Mary Cloake, John O'Kane, David Parnell and all at the Arts Council, Sinead Connolly and all at Dublin City Council Arts Office, Eugene Downes, Christine Sisk and all at Culture Ireland, Willie White, Nora Hickey M'Sichili, Fergus Hannigan and all at the Mermaid Arts Centre, Bríd Dukes, Niamh Honer and Kerry Hendley and all at the Civic Theatre, Niamh O'Donnell, Willie White and all at the Project Arts Centre, Emer McGowan and all at Draíocht, Tanya Tillett, Pat Laffan, Darren Healy, David Pearse, Feidlim Cannon, Holly Ní Chiarda and all those who have helped Fishamble with the production since this publication went to print.

Sean McLoughlin wishes to thank Ray and Rita McLoughlin and little Joe Ray Gavin for all their support.

Staff

Artistic Director	Jim Culleton
General Manager	Orla Flanagan
Literary Manager	Gavin Kostick
Office & Production Coordinator	Eva Scanlan

Board
Peter Finnegan, Caroline Gray, Eoin Kennelly (Chair), Siobhan Maguire, Stuart McLaughlin, Vincent O'Doherty, Andrew Parkes, Grace Perrott.

Fishamble: The New Play Company
Shamrock Chambers, 1/2 Eustace Street, Dublin 2, Ireland
Tel: +353-1-670 4018, fax: +353-1-670 4019
E-mail: info@fishamble.com
www.fishamble.com
www.facebook.com/fishamble
www.twitter.com/fishamble

Big Ole PIECE OF Cake

by **Sean McLoughlin**

The production runs without an interval and lasts approximately 80 minutes.
Setting: Wicklow, 2009.

Cast (in order of appearance)

Clarence	Mark Lambert
Colin	Ian-Lloyd Anderson
Ray	Joe Hanley

Director	Jim Culleton
Set Designer	Sinead O'Hanlon
Costume Designer	Donna Geraghty
Lighting Designer	Mark Galione
Sound Designers	Ivan Birthistle & Vincent Doherty
Producer	Orla Flanagan
Dramaturgical Support	Gavin Kostick
Production Manager	Des Kenny
Marketing & Production Coordinator	Eva Scanlan
Stage Director	Paula Tierney
Stage Manager	Andréa Laurent
Publicity	Zoetrope
Graphic Design	Gareth Jones
Photography	Patrick Redmond
Set Construction	Shadow Creations
Fight Director	James Cosgrave

Big Ole Piece of Cake was first produced by **Fishamble: The New Play Company**.
The production premiered on 2nd November 2010 at the Civic Theatre, Dublin.

About Fishamble: The New Play Company

Fishamble is an award-winning, internationally acclaimed company, dedicated to the discovery, development and production of new work for the Irish stage. Over the past 22 years, the Company has produced numerous plays by first-time and established playwrights. Fishamble has brought this work to audiences throughout Ireland as well as to England, Scotland, USA, Canada, Bulgaria, Romania, Turkey, France, Germany, Iceland and the Czech Republic.

Recent & Future Work
Recent work by Fishamble includes *Turning Point* in association with Arts & Disability Ireland (presented in Ireland and Washington DC), *The Pride of Parnell Street* by Sebastian Barry (on tour in Ireland and to the UK, France, Germany and the US), *Handel's Crossing* by Joseph O'Connor (on board the Jeanie Johnston as part of the Dublin Handel Festival), *Strandline* by Abbie Spallen, *Noah and the Tower Flower* by Sean McLoughlin (on tour to Bulgaria and Romania), *Rank* by Robert Massey (Dublin and London), and *Forgotten* by Pat Kinevane (on tour to over 50 Irish venues, 8 European cities and New York, Washington D.C. and Boston).

Future projects include collaborations with St Francis Hospice and RTÉ Radio, as well as *Silent,* a new play by Pat Kinevane (which was recently showcased as part of the Ulster Bank Dublin Theatre Festival), and new plays under commission from Sebastian Barry, Gavin Kostick, Gina Moxley and Rosaleen McDonagh.

Training, Development & Mentoring Schemes
As part of its commitment to developing new work for the theatre, Fishamble regularly presents workshops, discussions and seminars, as well as in-house and public readings of new work. Over the past decade, Fishamble has provided dramaturgical, training and mentoring support to playwrights and other theatre artists.

Current initiatives include: the Company's ongoing range of playwriting courses in Dublin and off-site for literary and arts festivals nationwide; the annual *Fishamble New Writing Award* at Absolut Fringe; *The New Play Clinic*, which supports new plays by theatre artists; *Show in a Bag* which creates new plays for actors and showcases them in association with the Irish Theatre Institute and Absolut Fringe; training by Fishamble as *Theatre Company in Association* at UCD Drama Studies Centre; *Mentoring Schemes* in Kildare and Fingal for emerging playwrights and directors.

> **'Fishamble is to be congratulated on bringing original material to the public. It is ploughing a risky furrow to produce fresh, innovative and modern Irish writing for the theatre.'**
> Mary McAleese, *President of Ireland*

> **'Without Fishamble, Irish theatre would be anaemic'**
> Brian Friel

Previous Productions of New Plays

2010
Turning Point by John Austin Connolly,
Steve Daunt*, Stephen Kennedy,
Rosaleen McDonagh
Forgotten (revival)

2009
Strandline by Abbie Spallen
The Pride of Parnell Street by Sebastian Barry
(revival)
Forgotten by Pat Kinevane (revival)
Handel's Crossing by Joseph O'Connor
Noah and the Tower Flower by Sean
McLoughlin (revival)

2008
Forgotten by Pat Kinevane (revival)
The Pride of Parnell Street by Sebastian Barry
(revival)
Rank by Robert Massey

2007
The Pride of Parnell Street by Sebastian Barry
Noah and the Tower Flower by Sean
McLoughlin*
Forgotten by Pat Kinevane

2006
Monged by Gary Duggan (revival)
Whereabouts – a series of short, site-specific
plays by Shane Carr*, John Cronin*, John
Grogan*, Louise Lowe, Belinda McKeon*,
Colin Murphy*, Anna Newell*, Jack Olohan*,
Jody O'Neill*, Tom Swift and Jacqueline
Strawbridge*
Forgotten by Pat Kinevane (work-in-progress)

The Gist of It by Rodney Lee***2005**
Monged by Gary Duggan*
She Was Wearing... by Sebastian Barry, Maeve
Binchy, Dermot Bolger, Michael Collins, Stella
Feehily, Rosalind Haslett, Roisin Ingle*, Marian
Keyes* and Gavin Kostick

2004
Pilgrims in the Park by Jim O'Hanlon
Tadhg Stray Wandered In by Michael Collins

2003
Handel's Crossing by Joseph O'Connor,
The Medusa by Gavin Kostick, *Chaste Diana*
by Michael West and *Sweet Bitter* by Stella
Feehily (a season of radio plays)
Shorts by Dawn Bradfield*, Aino Dubrawsky*,
Simon O'Gorman*, Ciara Considine*, Tina
Reilly*, Mary Portser, Colm Maher*, James
Heaney*, Tara Dairman*, Lorraine McArdle*,
Talaya Delaney*, Ger Gleeson*, Stella Feehily*
and Bryan Delaney*
The Buddhist of Castleknock by Jim O'Hanlon
(revival)

2002
Contact by Jeff Pitcher and
Gavin Kostick
The Buddhist of Castleknock by
Jim O'Hanlon*
Still by Rosalind Haslett*

2001
The Carnival King by Ian Kilroy*
Wired to the Moon by Maeve
Binchy, adapted by Jim Culleton

2000
Y2K Festival: Consenting Adults
by Dermot Bolger, *Dreamframe*
by Deirdre Hines, *Moonlight and
Music* by Jennifer Johnston, *The
Great Jubilee* by Nicholas Kelly*,
Doom Raider by Gavin Kostick,
Tea Set by Gina Moxley

1999
The Plains of Enna by
Pat Kinevane
True Believers by Joseph O'Connor

1998
The Nun's Wood
by Pat Kinevane*

1997
From Both Hips by Mark O'Rowe*

1996
The Flesh Addict by Gavin Kostick

1995
Sardines by Michael West
Red Roses and Petrol by Joe
O'Connor*

1994
Jack Ketch's Gallows Jig
by Gavin Kostick

1993
Buffalo Bill Has Gone To Alaska
by Colin Teevan
The Ash Fire by Gavin Kostick
(revival)

1992
The Ash Fire by Gavin Kostick*
The Tender Trap by Michael West

1991
Howling Moons/Silent Sons by
Deirdre Hines*
This Love Thing by Marina Carr

1990
Don Juan by Michael West

* denotes first play by a new playwright as part of Fishamble Firsts

Sean McLoughlin Author

As a young boy growing up in Artane, Sean wrote compulsively, winning many awards for his poetry and short stories. He began writing plays seriously when he was twenty eight, much due to the encouragement of the playwright Aodhan Madden. *Noah and the Tower Flower* was his first play, and was produced by Fishamble: The New Play Company at the Axis Theatre, Ballymun in April 2007, for which Sean received The Irish Times Best New Play Award and the Stewart Parker Trust Award. Fishamble subsequently commissioned Sean to develop *Big Ole Piece of Cake.*

Sean is currently developing a full-length screenplay, and has just completed a short film called *White Lady in the Window* for Samson Films.

Ian-Lloyd Anderson Colin

Ian-Lloyd Anderson graduated from the Gaiety School of Acting in 2007 and since then he has gone on to perform in theatres around Ireland. His theatre work includes the Abbey Theatre's productions of *Macbeth* and *The Resistable Rise of Arturo Ui*, directed by Jimmy Fay, and *The Rivals* directed by Patrick Mason. He also performed in Livin' Dred Theatre Company's *Observe the Sons of Ulster Riding Towards the Somme* directed by Padraic McIntyre, *End Time*, directed by John Delaney at the Project Arts Centre, and *Danti Dan,* directed by David Horan with Gallowglass Theatre Company. Most recently he played Hardress Gregan in *The Colleen Bawn* with Bedrock Theatre Company and the Project Arts Centre.

Ian has also worked in film and television. He appeared as Simon Owens in Series 6 of *The Clinic*, directed by Declan Eames. He also played Jake in *Dorothy Mills* directed by Agnes Merlet, and appeared in TG4's *The Wild Colonial Boy.*

Joe Hanley Ray

Joe's theatre work includes *The Plough and the Stars, The Playboy of the Western World* by Roddy Doyle and Bisi Adigun at the Abbey Theatre, *The Shawshank Redemption* (Gaiety Theatre, West End, national tour), *Juno and The Paycock* (Art NI and Cork Opera House, national tour), *Over and Out* (Lane Productions), *Homeland* by Paul Mercier (Abbey Theatre). Other theatre credits include *The Lieutenant of Inishmore* (Town Hall Theatre, Galway), Rough Magic's *Take Me Away* (Dublin, Edinburgh, Germany, London) which won the 2005 Stewart Parker Award and an Edinburgh Fringe First, *A Little Bit of Blue, One Flew Over The Cuckoos Nest, Twelve Angry Men* (Lane Productions), *Rap Eire, Much Ado About Nothing* (Bickerstaffe), *The Plough and the Stars* (Gaiety), *The Importance of Being Earnest* (Town Hall Theatre), *As You Like It* (Druid), *Massive Damages* (Passion Machine), *The Playboy of the Western World, As You Like It, Macbeth* (Second Age) and *Romeo and Juliet* (Gate Theatre).

Film and television credits include *Dorothy Mills, Murphy's Law, Single Handed, Batman Begins, The Front Line, Adam and Paul, Veronica Guerin, How Harry became a Tree, The Count of Monte Cristo, Flick, Agnes Browne, Run of the Country, Michael Collins, Empire* (ABC), *Prosperity, Stardust* and *Fair City.*

Sean McLoughlin   Ian-Lloyd Anderson   Joe Hanley   Mark Lambert   Jim Culleton

Mark Lambert Clarence

At Project Arts Centre: *The Last Days of Judas Iscariot*, also Rough Magic's *Don Carlos* and *Life is A Dream*. At the Abbey Theatre: *The Gigli Concert, Ariel, Observe the Sons of Ulster Marching Towards the Somme, Barbaric Comedies*. At the Gate: *Molly Sweeney, The Weir, Festen, The Three Sisters, Spirit of Annie Ross, Aristocrats, Month in the Country*. At Garter Lane: *Brighton* by Jim Nolan. In England: *Our Country's Good, Recruiting Officer, Ourselves Alone* (Royal Court), *All's Well That Ends Well* (RSC and Gielgud), *The Memory of Water,* (Vaudeville), *Dancing at Lughnasa* (Garrick), *Juno and The Paycock* (Wyndhams and Olivier Nomination), *Commedians* and *Long Days Journey Into Night* (Young Vic).
TV includes: *Cracker, Frost, Dalziel and Pascoe, Roy, Sharpes, Rifles, Vanity Fair, Bottom, Bloody Sunday, Tudors* and recently *Raw*. Film includes: *Veronica Guerin, Borstal Boy, Prayer for The Dying, Jude.*
Also directed productions for The Abbey, Royal Lyceum, Edinburgh, Opera House Belfast, Prime Cut, Tricycle Theatre, Storytellers and BBC Radio.

Jim Culleton Director

Jim is the Artistic Director of Fishamble: The New Play Company for which he most recently directed *Forgotten* by Pat Kinevane (on tour to over 50 Irish venues, 8 European countries and recently to New York, Boston and Washington DC), the multi award-winning *The Pride of Parnell Street* by Sebastian Barry (Irish tour, London, New Haven, Paris, Wiesbaden, New York), *Strandline* by Abbie Spallen, *Handel's Crossing* by Joseph O'Connor (Dublin Handel Festival), the multi award-winning *Noah and the Tower Flower* by Sean McLoughlin (Dublin, Bulgaria, Romania), *Rank* by Robert Massey (Dublin Theatre Festival and London), short plays for the award-winning *Whereabouts,* and the award-winning *Monged* by Gary Duggan (Irish and UK tour).
He has also directed for the Abbey/Peacock, 7:84 (Scotland), Project Arts Centre, Amharclann de hIde, Amnesty International, Pigsback, Tinderbox, The Passion Machine, The Ark, Second Age, RTÉ Radio 1, The Belgrade, Semper Fi, TNL Canada, Scotland's Ensemble @ Dundee Rep, Draíocht, Barnstorm, Roundabout, TCD School of Drama, the Irish Council for Bioethics, Origin (New York) and RTÉ lyric fm.
He most recently directed *Boss Grady's Boys* by Sebastian Barry for Noel Pearson at the Gaiety, *Turning Point* for Fishamble/ADI in Dublin and Washington DC, and *Bookworms* by Bernard Farrell for the Abbey. Current projects include *Silent* by Pat Kinevane and a range of training, mentoring and development projects, all for Fishamble.

Orla Flanagan Producer

Orla resumed the role of General Manager at Fishamble in 2008 following the completion of a Fellowship in Arts Management at the John F. Kennedy Centre for the Performing Arts in Washington D.C., for which she was awarded the Diageo Sponsored Fulbright Award for the Performing and Visual Arts. Other Fishamble productions she has produced since joining the Company in 2005 include *The Pride of Parnell Street*, *Handel's Crossing*, *Rank*, *Noah and the Tower Flower*, *The Gist of It*, *Forgotten*, *Monged* and the site-specific, multi-writer production of *Whereabouts (The Irish Times* Theatre Award winner 2006). From 2001-2005 she was the Literary Officer at the Abbey Theatre. She has also worked as Marketing Administrator at the National Concert Hall in Dublin and has produced a number of shows for the Dublin Fringe Festival. In 2005, she worked as a trainee dramaturg at the Sundance Theatre Lab, Utah, and the Schaubuhne's Festival of International New Drama '05, Berlin.

Des Kenny Production Manager

Credits include *Far Away*, *Urban Ghosts*, *Shooting Gallery*, *Wedding Day at the Cromagnons and This is our Youth* for Bedrock, *The Pride of Parnell Street*, *Noah and the Tower Flower*, *Pilgrims in the Park*, *Tadhg Stray Wandered In*, *The Gist Of It* and *Monged* for Fishamble, *Alone It Stands* for Lane Productions and Yew Tree Theatre Company, *Triple Espresso* and *The Shawshank Redemption* for Lane Productions, *Dublin by Lamplight*, *Mud* and *Everyday* for The Corn Exchange, *Sleeping Beauty* for Landmark/Helix and *How Many Miles to Babylon?*, *Macbeth*, *Othello*,*The Merchant of Venice*, *Doll's House* and *Hamlet* for Second Age and most recently, *Colleen Bawn* for Project Arts Centre/Civic Theatre/Bedrock.

Sinead O'Hanlon Set Designer

Sinead's designs for theatre include: *The Christmas Orchestra* and *Beware the Storybook Wolves* for The Ark, *Lizzie Lavelle and the Vanishing of Emlyclough*, *The Yokohama Delegation*, *The Butterfly Ranch* and *Candide* for The Performance Corporation, *Free to be...You and Me* for Team Theatre, *The Grown Ups* for The Peacock, *Mrs. Warren's Profession* for Cork Opera House, *The Factory Girls* for The Lyric Theatre, *Kvetch* for the Kilkenny Arts Festival, *Scenes from a Water Cooler* and *Four Storeys* for Gúna Nua Theatre Company.

Her designs for television include *The Sunday Game*, *Storylane* , *Watch Your Language*, *Winning Streak* and *That's all we've got time for*. Sinead previously designed set and costume for *Noah and the Tower Flower* by Sean McLoughlin.

Mark Galione Lighting Designer

Mark's designs in Ireland include works for Irish Modern Dance Theatre, Cois Ceim, Dance Theatre of Ireland, The Peacock, Fíbín, Hands Turn, Classic Stage Ireland, Barabbas, Holocaust Memorial Day at The Waterfront, Vesuvius, The Ark, Guna Nua, The Civic, Theatre Luvett and Barnstorm. In England his lighting designs included work for Nigel Charnock, Emilyn Claid, Ricochet, Small Axe, Gaby Agis, The Royal Ballet, Sherman Theatre and Soho Theatre Companies. For Fishamble he has lit *The Y2K Festival*, *Shorts*, *Still*, *Pilgrims In The Park*, *Monged*, *Tadgh Stray Wondered In*, *Noah and The Tower Flower*, *Rank* and *The Pride of Parnell Street*.

Ivan Birthistle & Vincent Doherty Sound Designers

Vincent and Ivan work together on an ongoing collaborative basis.
Past work includes: *Rank, Noah and the Tower Flower, The Gist of It, Monged* and *Tadgh Stray Wandered In* (Fishamble); *No Escape, Playboy of the Western World, Saved, The Alice Trilogy* and *True* West (The Abbey); *Swimming With My Mother, As You Are/Faun, Boxes* (Coisceim); *The Sanctuary Lamp* and *Honour* (B'spoke); *The Absence of Women, The Beauty Queen of Leenane, Homeplace, Dancing at Lughnasa, Much Ado About Nothing, Shadow of a Gunman* and *True West* (The Lyric); *Freefall, Mud, Foley* and *Lolita* (The Corn Exchange); *This Is Our Youth, Wedding Day at the Cro-Magnons', Roberto Zucco, This is Not a Life, Beckett's Ghosts, Shooting Gallery, Far Away* and *The Massacre @ Paris* (Bedrock); *Dying City, Pentecost* (Rough Magic); *Miss Julie* and *Blackbird* (Landmark); *Ladies and Gents, God's Grace, Adrenalin* and *Slaughter* (Semper-Fi).

Donna Geraghty Costume Designer

Donna Geraghty is a costume assistant in the costume department of the Abbey Theatre. Her freelance costume design work includes *No Escape* (the Peacock Theatre); *The Townlands of Brazil* (Axis Theatre); *End Time, Playground* and *Olive Skin, Blood Mouth* (The Gaiety School of Acting Degree shows); *Red Light Winter, How to Act around Cops and Shooters* (Purple Heart Theatre Company); *One for Sorrow and Two for a Girl* (Skipalong Theatre Company). Donna Geraghty is a graduate of the National College of Art and Design and Inchicore College of Further Education.

Paula Tierney Stage Director

Paula has previously worked with Fishamble on *True Believers* and *The Nun's Wood*. A graduate of UCC, Paula has worked on productions for Barabbas, Bickerstaffe, Calypso, Coiscéim, Druid Theatre Company, Everyman Palace Cork, Galloglass, The Gate Theatre, Gúna Nua, Galway Arts Festival, Kilkenny Arts Festival, Macnas, Pan Pan, The Peacock, Rough Magic and Second Age. She has toured nationally and internationally with Opera Theatre Company, Rough Magic and Druid.
She has been Stage Director at Buxton and Covent Garden Opera Festivals and at home for Opera Ireland and Wexford Festival Opera. Paula has also worked with *Après Match* and *Podge and Rodge* on their live theatre shows. In 2006 she called the opening ceremony of *The Ryder Cup* and toured to Kosovo with Traverse Theatre.
Recent productions include *The Walworth Farce*; US tour (Druid), *The Importance of Being Earnest* and *Phaedra* (Rough Magic).

Andréa Laurent Stage Manager

Andréa Laurent graduated in 2001 from the National College of Art and Design, with a degree in Fine Art, Sculpture. She began her stage management career in Paris with *Monty Python's Flying Circus* (in French) touring to London and Dublin. She then worked in stage management with Andrew's Lane Theatre and Lane Productions. Productions included *I Keano* touring in Ireland, *Tom Crean Antarctic Explorer, Triple Espresso, The Flags* and *Deadline*. She has been part of the stage management team in several productions in the Abbey and Peacock Theatres since 2007. Productions include *Woman and Scarecrow, Fool for Love, The Burial at Thebes, The Brothers Size, Happy Days, Ages of the Moon* and *The Playboy of the Western World*.

The Irish people have been let down by the banks, the construction industry and the Church, but Ireland's cultural industry has not failed the country.

Neil Jordan

The Arts are a necessity. Not a luxury.
The Arts are an asset. Not an overhead.

National Campaign for the Arts. **Visit ncfa.ie to see what you can do.**

Presented by Gúna Nua Theatre Company

Little Gem
by Elaine Murphy

The multi award winning, international, hit show is on tour throughout Ireland. Don't miss it!

"...as hilarious as it is poignant"
The Sunday Times

"...intimately told and beautifully acted"
The New York Times

" ★★★★★ ... a tiny treasure ..."
Time Out, London

"... impressive"
Sunday Independent

13–16 Oct. **Garter Lane, Waterford** www.garterlane.ie
18–19 Oct. **Town Hall, Galway** www.tht.ie
20–22 Oct. **Glor, Ennis** www.glor.ie
26–27 Oct. **Ramor Theatre, Cavan** www.ramortheatre.com
3–6 Nov. **Hawk's Well, Sligo** www.hawkswell.com
9–11 Nov. **Solstice Navan** www.solsticeartscentre.com
12–14 Nov. **Riverbank, Newbridge** www.riverbank.ie
15–20 Nov. **The Mill, Dundrum** www.milltheatre.com
29 Nov–1 Dec. **Pavilion, Dun Laoghaire** www.pavilliontheatre
2–4 Dec. **Wexford Opera House** www.wexfordoperahouse.ie

Take a bow!

The arts really matter to us in Ireland; they are a big part of people's lives, the country's single most popular pursuit. Our artists interpret our past, define who we are today, and imagine our future. We can all take pride in the enormous reputation our artists have earned around the world.

The arts play a vital role in our economy, and smart investment of taxpayers' money in the arts is repaid many times over. The dividends come in the form of a high value, creative economy driven by a flexible, educated, innovative work force, and in a cultural tourism industry worth €2.4 billion directly a year.

The Arts Council is the Irish Government agency for funding and developing the arts. Arts Council funding from the taxpayer, through the Department of Tourism, Culture and Sport, for 2010 is €69.15 million, that's less than €1 a week for every household.

So, at the end of your next great theatre performance, don't forget the role you played and take a bow yourself!

Find out what's on at
www.events.artscouncil.ie

You can find out more about the arts here:
www.artscouncil.ie

BIG OLE PIECE OF CAKE

Sean McLoughlin

For 1989 and the colour Yellow

Characters

CLARENCE, *sixty-three, slightly overweight with a grey beard and a full head of grey hair*

COLIN, *twenty-nine, tall and rigid, with rusty-coloured hair, cropped*

RAY, *forty-two, tallish with a wiry build. His hair is red and is thinning*

Both Colin and Ray have scraggly beards that are about two weeks old.

This text went to press before the end of rehearsals and so may differ slightly from the play as performed.

Scene One

*A country cottage. Two armchairs and a couch, centre stage.
Between the armchair and the couch there is a big log of wood
painted tar black. This is used as a table. An old black stove at
the back of the stage. A silver bucket containing wood blocks
and black prongs rests on the ground to the right of the stove.
On the back wall there is a painting of the Burren in County
Clare. It's not a particularly good painting. The back walls are
bilious green. On the wall behind the couch there is a large
Austrian wall clock. Below the clock there is a small cabinet,
above which is a record player. There is an exit, stage left and
stage right. The exit stage left leads to the kitchen, which we
cannot see. The exit to the right leads to a bedroom and the
toilet, which we cannot see.*

Enter CLARENCE *holding two brown grocery bags. He walks
through the room and exits stage left. A few seconds later*
COLIN *enters the room. He is holding an off-licence bag
containing a two-litre bottle of cider. He is wearing a yellow
snorkel jacket, jeans and yellow runners. He starts taking in the
cottage. He is fascinated by the place. There is a big grin on his
face. We hear the chink of cups.*

COLIN. Phat crib, Clarence!

CLARENCE (*offstage*). What was that?

COLIN. Phat crib! (*Short pause.*) Nice place ye have here.

CLARENCE. Aw, thank you.

    COLIN *nods a couple of times.*

COLIN. Mad cosy.

    COLIN *continues to take in the cottage. We hear a kitchen
    cupboard being closed.*

    Check it out, Ray. (*Dumps his bag down on the couch.*)

    Silence.

(*Stevie Wonder voice*.) Big ole piece of cake!

CLARENCE *enters the room, laughing. It's a very distinct laugh. In one hand,* CLARENCE *holds three cups and in the other, a bottle of Paddy's whiskey.*

That's some laugh ye have, Clarence.

CLARENCE (*putting bottle down on table*). Aw sure, don't I know. (*Short pause*.) Where's the other one?

COLIN. Out lookin' at the stars.

CLARENCE. Still?

COLIN *nods his head yes*.

Must really love the stars.

COLIN *gives two small nods*.

COLIN (*pointing at blue cup*). Can I have the blue one, please?

CLARENCE. Aw! Course ya can, here.

CLARENCE *hands it to him like he's presenting him with a trophy.*

COLIN. Tank *you*.

CLARENCE. You're welcome.

CLARENCE *puts the two cups he is holding down on the table and picks up the bottle of Paddy's.* COLIN *is inspecting the blue Boston cup.*

Came all the way from Boston, that.

COLIN. Yeah! (*Pointing at the name on the cup*.)

CLARENCE. That's the Boston cup! (*Uncaps bottle*.) Daughter was over there last summer. Brought that back for me.

COLIN. Lovely cup.

CLARENCE. Isn't it?

COLIN *nods a couple of times*.

COLIN. Like the little boats.

CLARENCE *laughs.* COLIN *nods and smiles at him.*

(*Reading an acronym on the cup.*) 'B-D-S.' What does that stand for?

CLARENCE. Couldn't tell ya. But I'd say the 'B' stands for Boston.

COLIN (*stretched*). Good call, Clarence. Good call!

CLARENCE *puts out the bottle to pour.*

CLARENCE. Put it out there now.

COLIN *puts out his cup for* CLARENCE *to pour.*

Say when.

CLARENCE *starts pouring whiskey in* COLIN*'s cup.*

COLIN. Sound!

CLARENCE *pulls the bottle away.* COLIN *steps back and sits down on the couch.* CLARENCE *looks towards the front door.*

CLARENCE *walks towards the front door. Just as he does,* RAY *walks in. He is holding a two-litre bottle of cider. He is wearing a dirty, light-blue bucket hat, a parka jacket, jeans and runners. The minute he walks into the room his eyes start wandering.*

CLARENCE. Ah, there ya are. Was gettin' worried about ya there.

CLARENCE *walks over to the cups.* RAY*'s eyes are fixed on the clock.*

Drop of whiskey... Ray, isn't it?

RAY *turns and nods yes.*

COLIN. Ray doesn't drink the spirits.

CLARENCE. Ya don't drink the spirits?

RAY *shakes his head.*

RAY. Poison.

CLARENCE. There's a lot out there that would agree with ya. (*Picks up a cup.*) Now. Pour meself a drop.

CLARENCE pours a large drink. COLIN starts chuckling.

COLIN. That's more than a bleedin' drop.

CLARENCE. Ah sure, I need to put a layer on the couple I had earlier on. Get awful groggy when ah have a couple, and then don't have a couple afterwards. Anyway, chin-chin.

CLARENCE drinks. He sighs. COLIN puts his cup down on the floor.

COLIN. Gonna have a bit of cider first.

CLARENCE gives him a small nod. COLIN pulls a two-litre bottle of cider out from his bag and sits. RAY is looking at the Austrian wall clock behind COLIN.

CLARENCE. Sit down, Ray.

RAY gives a small nod and goes to sit on the armchair closest to him.

Good lad.

COLIN uncaps the cider and takes a large slug.

I'll have a seat meself.

CLARENCE sits and lets out a groan. A short pause follows.

This is the way I want to go out, lads. Sitting in this very armchair… cup of whiskey in the hand.

COLIN. Go out where?

RAY. *Die!* Ye fuckin' donkey.

COLIN. Oh!

Pause.

COLIN starts looking around the room.

Love this cottage, I do. Absolutely love it!

CLARENCE gives him a small nod.

RAY. It's nice alrigh'.

COLIN. Isn't it?

RAY *gives a small nod.*

Mad country!

COLIN *takes another swig then puts his flagon down on the ground.*

CLARENCE. '*Phat crib!*'

COLIN *and* RAY *snigger.*

That's what ya called it.

COLIN. Yeah!

CLARENCE. 'Phat crib!'

RAY *and* COLIN *are still sniggering.*

I like that. Give us... (*Clicks his fingers a couple of times.*) the thing about the cake.

COLIN *leans in towards* CLARENCE, *eyes bulging.*

COLIN (*deep African-American voice*). Big ole piece of cake!

CLARENCE *starts laughing.*

D'ye hear the laugh on that? Ray?

RAY. I hear it, yeah.

COLIN. Sounds like... (*To himself.*) What does it sound like?

Pause.

CLARENCE. So did ye count them all?

COLIN *looks up to see who he is talking to.*

RAY. Talkin' about?

CLARENCE. The stars.

RAY. Oh.

COLIN. Fuckin' hape of them, isn't there? Why is that? Fuck-all in Dublin.

CLARENCE. Not as much light.

COLIN. Wha'?

CLARENCE. Less light! It's all the light…

COLIN *is dumbfounded*. CLARENCE *points at him*.

If you were to go up the Kippure mountain some night… and ya were to look down at the city, you'd see a big orange glow surrounding it. That's what blocks out all the stars.

RAY. He's righ'.

CLARENCE. More light, less stars.

COLIN. But the sky is the sky.

RAY. The light blocks out the sky!

CLARENCE. The expanse of it.

RAY. Yeah. The expanse of it.

COLIN. Bu'…

RAY. He's righ', Colin! More light, less stars. Now, will ye just drop it!

RAY *shakes his head and uncaps his cider*.

COLIN. Relax, Ray.

RAY. Keep goin' on about it. Very simple.

RAY *takes a swig from his cider*. COLIN *flaps his lips*. CLARENCE *points at the cup on the table*.

CLARENCE. Sure, use the cup there.

RAY. Ah, yer alrigh'.

RAY *puts his flagon down and then goes through his jacket pockets. He takes out twenty Pall Mall and a pink lighter. He suddenly freezes*.

Alrigh' to have a smoke, Clarence?

CLARENCE. Fire away.

RAY *takes a cigarette out of the box*.

Pall Mall.

RAY. D'ye want one?

CLARENCE. No no. Not a smoker.

COLIN. Cheapest smokes out there.

CLARENCE. That right?

COLIN. Yeah.

CLARENCE (*points at* RAY). I'll go and get ya an ashtray.

RAY *nods.* CLARENCE *stands up. He groans as he does this. He puts his cup down on the wooden log.* COLIN *takes a slug from his cider.*

Are ya not drinking your whiskey?

COLIN. In a minute. Wouldn't have anythin' to mix it with, would ye?

CLARENCE. I would. I'll go and get that for ya now. And the ashtray!

COLIN. Thank you, Clarence.

CLARENCE. You're welcome. (*Just before exiting.*) Impeccable manners, doesn't he?

RAY. Ah, he's mannerly alrigh'.

Exit CLARENCE.

COLIN. Manners are essential!

CLARENCE (*offstage*). Now ya have it.

Silence.

RAY (*whispers*). Caravan out the back.

COLIN. Wha'?

RAY *puts a finger to his lips. We hear kitchen cupboards being opened.*

RAY (*whispers but stressing*). Caravan out the back.

COLIN. Yeah?

RAY *nods his head.*

RAY (*whispers*). Don't say nuttin' now.

> RAY *takes a swig from his cider.*

COLIN. Abou' wha'?

CLARENCE (*offstage*). Where's that bloody ashtray?

RAY (*whispered through gritted teeth*). The caravan! (*Shakes his head.*) We're gonna take the fuckin' thing.

COLIN (*joyful*). Are we?

RAY. Sssssssh. Yes.

> COLIN *is glowing.*

COLIN (*pointing at* RAY). I fucking love you I do. (*Stops pointing.*) Fuckin' love ye.

> RAY *gives him a sardonic look and then shakes his head, sighing.*

CLARENCE (*offstage*). Ah! There she is.

RAY (*hushed tone*). We have one of them hooks at the back of the car. Just lob it on and off we go.

COLIN. Fuckin' sweet.

RAY. Take that with us as well.

> RAY *nods at the wall clock.*

COLIN. Wha'?

RAY. Tha'.

> RAY *nods and points at the clock.* COLIN *turns around and looks at it.*

COLIN. Nice clock, alrigh'.

RAY. Mmmmmm.

> RAY *lights up a cigarette. Silence for a few seconds. He looks very happy.* COLIN *points at* RAY's *Pall Malls.*

COLIN. Can I get one of them off ye?

RAY. Leave ye a drag.

COLIN. Ah, Ray.

RAY. I told ye to ration, Colin! (*Quietens down.*) Fuckin' told ye! But ye smoked the lot of them like the retard ye are.

Silence.

Enter CLARENCE *a few seconds later, holding an ashtray and a bottle of TK Red Lemonade. He plonks it down on the log.*

CLARENCE. For you! (*Hands* RAY *ashtray.*) *And for you!*

RAY. Sound job.

Silence.

CLARENCE *sits.*

CLARENCE. So, lads. What part of the city are yez from?

COLIN. East Wall.

CLARENCE. East Wall!

COLIN. Yeah, d'ye know it?

CLARENCE. Do I know it? Sure, I used to teach across the road from it for nearly sixteen years. A lot of the lads I taught would of been from East Wall.

RAY. Joey's?

CLARENCE. That's the one. Did yaz go there yourselves, lads?

RAY. No.

CLARENCE. Up the road, was it?

COLIN. *You're* a teacher!

COLIN *gawks at him.*

Come on, Ray, are ye righ'.

COLIN *scoops up his flagon and stands. He steps away from his chair.*

RAY. Sit down, ye fool.

COLIN *stops. He has a grin on his face. He walks back to his seat but doesn't sit.*

CLARENCE. *Was*. Haven't taught in nearly… thirty years.

COLIN. Were ye strict?

CLARENCE. No.

COLIN. Go on out of tha'.

CLARENCE *has trouble getting the words out.*

CLARENCE. Wasn't. (*Short pause.*) Had this system, lads, right. You wanted to learn, ya sat up the front. You didn't want to learn, ya sat down the back.

RAY. Seems like a good system.

CLARENCE. And if I was hungover, you could sit wherever ya fucking wanted!

RAY *gives a small laugh.*

COLIN. Could ye smoke down the back?

CLARENCE. No.

Short pause.

COLIN. Could ye eat down the back?

CLARENCE. I'd allow it.

RAY. Sit down!

COLIN *slowly sits down, not taking his eyes off* CLARENCE *and grinning the whole time. He uncaps his flagon.*

CLARENCE. To be honest with yez, lads… I think I was a hell of a good teacher. (*Short pause.*) Made history interesting, ye see! Which is what it's all about.

RAY. You were a history teacher?

CLARENCE. I was. But going back to what I was saying… when I taught history… I… I… I didn't… I didn't teach it like most of the teachers out there teach it. Ye know. That… that… shitty, perfunctory way. Move on to the next chapter, lads, or… writing up a big whole load of notes on the blackboard! No! (*A beat.*) I turned it into a debate! Whatever

the topic. Whether it was… World War Two or…
Communism in Russia. Ya know. Why did Stalin want to
keep Communism all for himself? Why didn't he want to
spread it right throughout the world like Trotsky? Ended up
gettin' a pickaxe to the head in Mexico in 1940!

COLIN *bursts out laughing.*

COLIN. You on uppers, Clarence?

CLARENCE. 'Uppers'?

COLIN. Pills? Make ye mad hyped.

CLARENCE. Aw, I get like this sometimes when I'm… ya
know… the whiskey and the…

RAY (*to* COLIN). Yer some tulip, ye know that?

COLIN. Wha'?

RAY. Askin' the man somethin' like that.

COLIN. I was only messin' with him! I was only messin' with
ye, Clarence. Honest! Here! Have a few names for ye.

CLARENCE. Right?

Short pause.

COLIN. Gary Ceary.

RAY. He hasn't taught in over thirty years, Colin! Gary Ceary
would of been in bleedin' nappies when he stopped teachin'.

COLIN. Aw, yeah.

CLARENCE. Did a bit of subbin' for a few years down the
road, but sure… that doesn't really count, I suppose.

RAY. Steppin' in for teachers when they were sick, like?

CLARENCE. That's it.

Pause.

COLIN *takes a sup of his flagon, caps it and then puts it on
the floor.* RAY *looks at* CLARENCE. *He throws his head
back slightly as if to indicate to* CLARENCE *that he's about
to say something to him.*

RAY. Come here. Ye reckon Stalin was worse than Hitler?

CLARENCE. Killed twenty million of his own. Hitler never did that.

COLIN (*German accent, making Nazi salute*). Svine! Svine!

CLARENCE. That was Adolph alright.

RAY. Except Hitler would of done that. (*Flicks hand over shoulder.*) Not that. (*Makes Nazi salute.*)

CLARENCE. Ah, sure, he did that as well.

RAY. Did he?

CLARENCE *nods.*

CLARENCE. Whenever the storm troopers were passing.

RAY *shrugs and sticks out his lower lip.* COLIN *picks up the bottle of TK Red Lemonade and uncaps it. He pours the TK Red into his cup of whiskey.*

RAY. Betcha ye didn't know that Hitler was almost aborted.

CLARENCE. I didn't, no.

RAY. There ye go now.

CLARENCE. My God.

RAY. Ma pulled out at the last minute.

CLARENCE. Didn't know that now.

RAY. World would of been a different place if his ma went ahead with it. Or would it have been?

CLARENCE. Perhaps. (*Short pause.*) I think I might be in the presence of a fellow historian here, Colin.

RAY. Not at all. Just like watchin' documentaries.

COLIN. Loves watchin'… Ray! (*Pointing at the cigarette.*)

RAY *takes a final drag of the cigarette and then hands it out for* COLIN *to take.* COLIN *puts down his cup, walks over to* RAY *and takes it from him.*

Thanking you.

RAY *picks up his flagon, uncaps and takes a slug.* COLIN *puts the cigarette in his mouth, picks up the ashtray and then sits back down. He takes a long pull from the cigarette.*

This is what I would of been doin' if I was in your class. Smokin'! Down the back!

RAY *rolls his eyes. He takes a slug from his flagon.*

CLARENCE. And where would you of been sitting in the class, Ray?

RAY (*putting cap back on flagon*). Wouldn't of even been in the class. (*Puts flagon down on floor.*) Would of been in Barney's playin' Street Fighter! Self and Jay Kelly were fuckin' brilliant at that game. Swear to Jesus, Clarence. Use to get up to level eigh'. And with only three lives, that's all. (*A beat.*) 'Blow me a bubble, big boy!'(*They all laugh.*) There was this big Buddha in the game, righ'?

CLARENCE. Right.

RAY. Use to blow these bubbles. Big massive things. Soon as ye walked into them, floatin' over Samurais for miles.

CLARENCE. So while all those poor teachers in... what school did ya go to? Ya never told me.

RAY. North Strand Tech.

CLARENCE *nods a few times, smiling to himself.*

CLARENCE. So while all those poor teachers in North Strand Tech were worrying where ya were... the whole time ya were floating over Samurais.

RAY. Yeah.

CLARENCE. I love it.

RAY *nods to himself a couple of times. There's a few seconds of silence.*

Do yaz work, lads?

COLIN. Window cleaners!

CLARENCE. Yez are window cleaners?

COLIN. Professional window cleaners.

CLARENCE. *Professional* window cleaners.

COLIN. Yeah.

CLARENCE. Aw, the buckets and the… in the back seat of the car.

Short pause.

COLIN. Fifteen euro, front and back!

CLARENCE. Sounds reasonable.

COLIN. Bleedin' righ'. Bleedin' *Deliverance* charges twenty!

CLARENCE. 'Deliverance charges'…?

RAY. He's talkin' about a fella from the area. Does the window cleanin' as well.

CLARENCE *is still puzzled.*

Looks like somethin' from *Deliverance*. Mad hillbilly-lookin' character.

CLARENCE. Oh!

CLARENCE *starts laughing wildly.*

COLIN. What does that laugh sound like?!

CLARENCE. I thought you meant… delivery charges or something. (*Takes a sip from his whiskey. What he says next is straight to* COLIN.) So yez decided not to bring the ladder down? Just the buckets and rags.

COLIN. Don't have a ladder! That bastard brother of ours took it off us! Wanker! Thomas the Tank Engine!

RAY *is now staring at* COLIN.

Thinks he's an INLA man. Scumbag! He'll get his come-uppin's. (*To* RAY.) Won't he? (*Short pause.*) Wha'?

CLARENCE. Why did he take your ladder?

COLIN. Coz…

RAY. Wanted a loan of it, Clarence. Does a little bit on the side, ye know. Not like us. We're professionals. That righ', bro?

COLIN *nods*.

Doesn't like anyone gettin' the ladder. Mad precious about it. But sure... if we're down here for the day, we might as well give it to him. Let 'im make a few squid for himself.

CLARENCE. Ah, yeah. Sure, he's a brother.

RAY. True.

Pause.

CLARENCE. Still have your coats on, are yez cold?

RAY. Eh...

COLIN. Bit nippy, yeah.

CLARENCE. Sure, I'll stick on the stove, for God's sake. Should of said something to me.

CLARENCE *stands up. He puts his cup down on the log table and walks over to the stove.* COLIN *puts his cigarette out in the ashtray.*

COLIN. Use yer jacks, Clarence? Burstin'.

COLIN *stands up.* CLARENCE *points to the stage-left exit.*

CLARENCE. Second door.

COLIN. Good man.

COLIN *then walks over to* CLARENCE. *He pats him on the back.* CLARENCE *turns and looks at him.*

Yer a good oul skin, so ye are.

CLARENCE. Ahh, I do me best.

COLIN. Very friendly.

CLARENCE. Ah...

COLIN. Ye are though. All I did was give ye the thumbs-up – (*Gives* CLARENCE *the thumbs-up sign.*) in the car and sure ye walked over and started chattin' to us.

Exit COLIN, *stage left*.

RAY. Chancin' his arm, so he was. Looking for a lift back here.

CLARENCE. Not at all, not at all.

COLIN (*offstage*). He's windin' ye up, Clarence.

CLARENCE *looks out at* COLIN, *who is about to enter a room*.

CLARENCE. The other one, Colin!

COLIN (*offstage*). Wha'?

CLARENCE. The other door.

COLIN (*offstage*). Aw, this one?

CLARENCE. Yah.

CLARENCE *breaks a couple of sticks*.

And before I forget…

COLIN (*offstage*). What's the other one?

CLARENCE *gives a small chuckle*.

CLARENCE. My bedroom.

COLIN (*offstage*). Aw!

COLIN *shuts the door*. CLARENCE *goes to speak to* RAY *again*.

(*Offstage*.) Wouldn't want to be goin' in there!

CLARENCE *gives a small laugh*. RAY *shakes his head*. CLARENCE *tilts his head back and tells* RAY *what he has wanted to tell him the last few seconds, almost like a sigh*.

CLARENCE. Thank you very much for the lift, Ray.

RAY. Nay bother.

CLARENCE *bends down and picks up a stick*.

Need a hand?

CLARENCE. Do I look that old, do I?

CLARENCE *cracks the stick*.

RAY. What age are ye anyway? If ye don't mind me askin', that is.

CLARENCE. A six and a three. Sixty-three! (*Turns towards the stove.*) Gettin' feckin' old, so I am. (*Throws the stick into the stove. He shuts the door and starts to turn on the stove.*) The biggest surprise in a man's life is old age. (*Silence. Turns and faces* RAY.) Tolstoy said that.

RAY *nods a couple of times.*

RAY. Heard of 'im.

CLARENCE *gives a small nod. Short pause.* CLARENCE *walks to his seat.*

CLARENCE. So did yez go into McHugh's for a pint?

RAY *is puzzled.*

The pub yez were parked outside.

RAY. Eh... no. Just down here for the drive, Clarence, ye know.

CLARENCE *nods a couple of times.* RAY *looks at the painting on the back wall. We hear the toilet being flushed.*

What's that, Clarence?

CLARENCE. That's the Burren.

RAY. That the Burren?

CLARENCE. That's the Burren. Daughter painted that. (*Short pause.*) Whatcha think of it?

Enter a very hyped-up and excited COLIN.

COLIN. I have it! I have it! I bleedin' have it!

RAY. Have what? Ye goon.

COLIN *looks at him and shakes his head.*

CLARENCE. What do ya have, Colin?

COLIN. I know what ye laugh like. (*A beat.*) Ye laugh like a sea lion.

RAY *sniggers and then picks up his flagon.*

RAY. He does actually.

COLIN. Doesn't he? Ye laugh like a sea lion, Clarence.

CLARENCE (*little bit embarrassed*). Hmmmph.

> COLIN *looks at him and nods a couple of times. He then sits.* RAY *uncaps his flagon.*

COLIN. Big ole piece of cake!

> RAY *sniggers.* CLARENCE *gives a small laugh.*

> There! (*To* RAY.) D'ye hear it?

RAY (*sardonic*). Yeah. (*Rolls his eyes, then takes a slug from flagon.*) Fuckin' love a piece of cake now, so I would.

CLARENCE. Hungry, lads?

RAY. Little bit peckish, alrigh'.

COLIN. Fuckin' starvin'!

CLARENCE. Aw, for God's sake. Can't have that. Would yez have a bit of chicken, lads? Pile of chicken in there in the fridge. More than welcome to it.

COLIN. Mos' def! Mos' def!

RAY. That would be lovely, Clarence.

> CLARENCE *stands. He takes a sip of his whiskey.* COLIN *sits down.*

CLARENCE. So I laugh like a sea lion?

COLIN. Ye do.

> CLARENCE *puts down his cup. He titters to himself as he exits for the kitchen. We hear him humming a tune in the kitchen.*

RAY (*hushed tone*). Might not have to rob that caravan, Col.

COLIN. Wha'?

RAY (*hushed tone*). Oul codger's after takin' a shine to us. Might just let us stay there.

COLIN*'s mouth drops.*

COLIN. That'd be better. In and out of the gaff for food.

RAY *sniggers.*

RAY (*hushed tone*). No no no no. We're stickin' to the original plan. But just in case, righ', just in case... say nuttin' about what went down in the gaff!

COLIN *nods a couple of times.*

RAY *glares at* COLIN. COLIN *nods a couple of times again.* RAY *stands. He brushes himself down.*

COLIN. Fuckin' scumbag.

RAY. What?

COLIN. Thomas.

RAY. Oh.

A beat.

COLIN. Scumbag.

RAY. And here! Say nuttin' about being in Mountjoy. You're always at that.

COLIN *nods again.* RAY *stares at him for a second or two.*

Just usin' yer jacks, Clarence.

CLARENCE (*offstage*). Right ya be.

RAY *starts to exit. He points a finger at the wall clock as he exits.*

RAY. That's definitely an antique job.

Lights down.

Scene Two

The stage lights come up again. All three men are seated. On the log is a bowl containing the carcass of a chicken. Beside the bowl are several slices of brown bread, a carving knife and salt. RAY and COLIN are hunched over, scavenging the chicken which is laid before them on the wooden log. Their coats are now off and on their seats behind them. They are both wearing tracksuit tops. RAY slouches back in his armchair, stuffed from the food. CLARENCE sits upright with a cup of whiskey in his hand.

CLARENCE. My God, yez were hungry, lads.

RAY. Starvin' Marvin.

    RAY *pats his stomach.*

CLARENCE. Yes. (*Short pause.*) Look at him. Still eating.

COLIN (*mouth full*). Love chicken! Love it! (*Swallows what's in his mouth.*) Don't like it when it's hot. Hate the skin. Always tear it off. Eat it when it's cold, though. Eat it then. (*Picks up the carving knife and cuts himself a slice of brown bread.*) Love chicken! (*Puts bread into his mouth and starts eating it.*) African-Americans love their chicken!

CLARENCE. What was that?

COLIN. African-Americans love their chicken!

CLARENCE. That right?

    Short pause.

RAY. Colin here loves the blacks of America.

COLIN. African-Americans.

RAY. Please.

COLIN. Get it righ'.

    Short pause.

CLARENCE. Happy with Obama?

COLIN. Yes.

CLARENCE. 'Yes we can!'

COLIN *gives* CLARENCE *a moronic stare.*

That's what he said.

COLIN. Did he?

CLARENCE. He did.

RAY. Colin only likes the *African-Americans* who deal drugs and shoot people.

CLARENCE. Oh, right.

COLIN. I be bangin'! I be bangin'!

RAY (*sarcastic*). I be bangin'.

COLIN. Nidge! You betta shut yo mouth before I put a cap yo *Tupac*-wannabe ass.

CLARENCE *titters.*

RAY (*sarcastic*). I think I know about… two, maybe three Tupac songs.

COLIN. Ye know what it's from.

RAY *reaches down for his flagon.*

RAY. Seriously, Col – (*Uncapping flagon.*) that oul nigger talk is grand when yer with the jelly babies in Fairview park, but when yer with adults…

CLARENCE. Ah, I like it.

COLIN. Yeeeeee! Clarence likes it! Clarence is my homey.

CLARENCE. Well, I'm at home anyway.

RAY *takes a slug.* COLIN *reaches down for his already opened flagon.*

COLIN. Wash the oul chicken down.

CLARENCE. Good lad.

RAY *caps his flagon and then puts it down on the floor.*
COLIN *takes a big slug from his. He sighs.*

Short pause.

COLIN. All the homies in Oakland love their chicken.

CLARENCE. That right?

COLIN *nods yes. He then puts his flagon down.*

COLIN. If you're a snitch in Oakland and ye wanna cop
information to the Gards… ye get a bucket of chicken.

CLARENCE. 'A bucket of chicken'?

RAY. One of the KFC buckets.

CLARENCE. Oh, right. Because I had a ghastly vision there for
a second of someone being presented an actual bucket… a
work bucket… with a chicken in it.

RAY (*laughing*). A live chicken?

CLARENCE (*titters*). No, a dead one. But uncooked!

RAY. Uhhh.

COLIN *shakes his head.*

COLIN. You's are mad.

RAY. D'ye hear this? Should be in Grangegorman [*a mental
institute*].

Pause.

COLIN. Shut up, you.

RAY *gives him a darting look.*

Thank you for the food, Clarence.

CLARENCE. You're welcome. (*Pause.*) Never told me what ye
thought of the painting, Ray.

COLIN. What is it?

CLARENCE. The Burren.

RAY. Clare.

COLIN *stares at it*.

COLIN. Wouldn't want to live there.

CLARENCE. Jesus, no. (*Small pause*.) So what do ye think of it?

Short pause.

RAY. Yeah.

Short pause.

COLIN. Did *you* draw that?

RAY. It's a paintin', ye goon.

CLARENCE. Daughter painted it.

COLIN. The one that went to Boston?

CLARENCE. No, the other one. Aine. The younger lassie.

COLIN. Wha' age…

RAY. How did you know his daughter went to Boston? Ye obviously told 'im.

CLARENCE. While you were out stargazing.

RAY. Hmmph.

COLIN. What age is Aine?

CLARENCE. Oh… thirty-two? Thirty-two!

COLIN. And the other one? The one that went to Boston?

CLARENCE. Thirty-four!

CLARENCE *pours himself a drop of whiskey*.

COLIN *grins*.

COLIN. Good-lookin'?

CLARENCE. Nice-lookin' lassies alrigh'.

COLIN. Really?

CLARENCE. Aw, yeah. Particularly the younger one.

COLIN *grins at* RAY.

RAY. Don't say it.

COLIN. Any chance of settin' them up with me and Ray?

RAY. Fuckin' said it.

CLARENCE. Both taken, Colin.

COLIN. Ahhh.

RAY. Married?

CLARENCE. One is. The other is as good as.

COLIN. That's a pity now.

CLARENCE. Wouldn't of worked out anyway, Colin.

COLIN. Why not?

CLARENCE. Both of them are teachers. Sure, so was the wife.

COLIN. Ah, for God's sake.

RAY. Does she live here?

CLARENCE. Naw. Hmmph. No no no no. Lives up in Dublin. (*Pause.*) The cunt from Cavan!

COLIN *gives* RAY *a shocked look.*

RAY. Who?

CLARENCE (*clears his throat, a little bit ashamed*). The wife.

Short pause.

COLIN. Yez are obviously separated?

RAY. Don't be askin' the man that!

CLARENCE. Ah sure, if you're going to make a statement like that… (*Sighs, there follows a short pause.*) She didn't want any more children, lads. Two was enough for her. (*Away into thin air.*) Funny thing about it was… before the marriage she wanted a rake of them! Wanted a whole load of them!

COLIN. So… like…

CLARENCE *points at the bottle.* COLIN *gives him a puzzled look.*

Wha'?

CLARENCE. That's why she wouldn't give me another child. (*Cavan accent.*) 'I'm not bringing another child into this environment.'

COLIN *is still puzzled.*

She used my drinking as an excuse not to give me another child. And it would of been a son! I know it, lads! It would of been a son! (*A beat.*) Fuck it! (*Short pause.*) Wouldn't mind... all I was, was a binger. Midterm breaks and what have ya. The odd slip now, admittedly, but... ah, I was no Alex Higgins, that's for sure. Turned me into one, though! Ended up losing my job... drinking on park benches... wouldn't let me into the house when I was drinking, ye see, lads. And it wasn't like I was... All I'd do was... sit in the back room... drinking beer and chasers, listening to the wigs. That's all.

COLIN. They a band?

CLARENCE. That's what I call all the great classical composers.

Short pause.

COLIN. Righ'.

Short pause.

CLARENCE. Education department were pretty decent now, I have to say. Tried to set me up with another job in Donaghmede... (*Starts shaking his head.*) Had enough of Dublin by that stage. Packed a bag and headed down here to the mother's. Felt very guilty about it. Leaving my two lovely lassies.

RAY. She should of given ye a son, Clarence.

CLARENCE. She should of! She should of! Fucking cunt! Awful thing to say, I know but, sure... (*Short pause.*) The next one would of been a son! I know it, lads! You know when ya get that gut feelin'?

Short pause.

RAY. Still, ye have two daughters.

CLARENCE. That's true! That's true! I'll drink to that! (*Takes a sip*.) The older one still has issues with me I think. Left the house when she was around nine. (*Pause*.) Any children yourself, Ray?

RAY *shakes his head no*.

RAY. Well… not that I know of.

COLIN. Has a load of them scattered throughout the city.

RAY *looks at* CLARENCE *and shakes his head*.

RAY. Only child I have is him.

COLIN. Fug off.

Short pause.

CLARENCE. What about yourself?

COLIN. No, but I'd love to have one.

CLARENCE. Would ye?

COLIN *nods his head yes*.

COLIN. Little boy. Bowl haircut, little Nike runners.

CLARENCE *titters*.

Bring 'im everywhere, I would.

CLARENCE. Oakland being top of the list.

COLIN. Yeah! And Jamaica! Rastafari, dread-eye, jah live!

Short pause.

RAY. Tell Clarence what yer gonna call yer son.

COLIN. Animal! From *The Muppets,* like! Remember him?

COLIN *impersonates Animal playing the drums*.
CLARENCE *stares at him in disbelief. A short pause follows*.

CLARENCE. Ya can't call your son that, Colin.

COLIN. Why not? I like it!

CLARENCE. But your son won't! He'll end up resenting ya.

COLIN. Wha'?

RAY. Of all the names that are out there… Philip, Paul, John…

COLIN. I'm callin' 'im Animal!

RAY. Ye are an animal.

CLARENCE. And and… what are ya gonna call yer daughter.

COLIN. Beyoncé.

CLARENCE. Beyoncé! That's a bit of an improvement now, I have to say. Where's that name from, anyway? Is that a French name?

RAY. Call 'er Miss Piggy.

COLIN *looks at* RAY *and shakes his head*.

COLIN. I don't know where it's from, Clarence. Just know the singer Beyoncé.

RAY. I really think ye should call 'er Miss Piggy, Colin. I mean, if yer gonna call…

COLIN. I think ye should take off yer hat!

RAY *gives* COLIN *an evil stare*.

Tell 'im to take off his hat, Clarence.

Short pause.

RAY. Think yer smart, do ye? Think yer smart?! I'll put ye into that back wall, so I will!!

COLIN. Ye wish.

RAY. I fuckin' will!

CLARENCE. Ah now, lads lads lads lads. (*Short pause.*) Didn't bring yez in here to fight. Brought yez in for a drink and a bit of conversation. Not to fight.

COLIN. He started it.

CLARENCE (*waving both hands*). D… d… d. Doesn't matter who started it. Let's just put it to rest now. (*Short pause*.) Shake hands there now, lads. (*Short pause*.) Come on now, shake hands.

COLIN *leans over and puts his hand out*. RAY *doesn't shake it*. COLIN *pulls back*.

COLIN. Doesn't wanna shake me hand.

RAY. No need to shake hands. It's cool.

CLARENCE. Sure, just shake his hand anyway.

RAY *sighs*.

RAY. Here.

RAY *leans forward and puts out his hand*. COLIN *shakes it*.

CLARENCE. That's better. (*Short pause*.) Yez are brothers, lads. Yez shouldn't be fighting.

Pause.

RAY. Just goin' outside for a smoke, Clarence.

RAY *stands up*.

CLARENCE. Sure, have it here?

RAY. Prefer to have it outside.

RAY *starts exiting*.

CLARENCE. Yer not still angry, are ye?

RAY. No, no.

CLARENCE. Go through all the Bruce wars.

RAY *stops and gives him a puzzled look*.

That's what I always do when I'm angry, or when something's troubling me. 1315, Battle of Carrick Fergus. 1316, second battle of Athenry…

RAY. I'm not angry, Clarence.

CLARENCE. Good lad.

Exit RAY.

COLIN. Don't mind 'im. (*Uncaps cider.*) Moody cunt. (*Takes a swig. There follows a short pause. He starts putting the cap back on.*) Wasn't so moody he'd look a lot younger. Have a guess what age he is, Clarence.

CLARENCE. Ohhh…

COLIN. Forty-two! Doesn't look it, does he? Looks about fifty!

CLARENCE. Ahh, I wouldn't say that now.

COLIN. Ye would if I whipped off that hat!

CLARENCE (*almost whispering*). Losing the hair, is he?

COLIN. Big time! Sure, that's why he wears the hat.

CLARENCE *puts a finger to his lips.*

(*Whispering now.*) Can't go anywhere without it.

COLIN *gives one of his goofy laughs.*

CLARENCE. Ya shouldn't be teasin' him about that now, Colin.

COLIN. Pppph. If he's gonna keep slaggin' me the whole time… callin' me a retard.

CLARENCE. I know, I know, but…

COLIN. Calls me that every day, so he does.

CLARENCE. He shouldn't.

COLIN. Does though. Every day! Highly offensive. (*Pause.*) I'd love to be able to do somethin' brilliant! Somethin' absolutely fantastic! So I could just turn around and say… 'Can you do that, can ye?! No, ye can't! I can do that though!' Nuttin' I can fuckin' do though. Fuckin' useless.

CLARENCE. Ah, you're being too hard on yourself now, Colin.

COLIN. True though.

CLARENCE. There must be something you're good at.

Short pause.

COLIN. Drinkin' flagons. That's about it. Is there a competition for drinkin' flagons?

CLARENCE. There is that thing in Germany.

COLIN. Aw! Where they drink the big mad fuckin' tankard things.

CLARENCE. That's the one.

COLIN. Fuckin' huge, them things are!

CLARENCE. October Fest! That's what it's called. They only drink beer though. Strictly beer.

COLIN. Wouldn't stop me from goin'. (*Short pause*.) That's another thing about Ray! Never wants to go anywhere.

CLARENCE. Sure, yez are down here.

COLIN. I'm talkin' about foreign countries, like. Like Jamaica! Been askin' 'im for years to go to Jamaica. Always the same answer. (*Impersonates* RAY.) 'Next year, next year.' Given up askin' 'im.

CLARENCE. Sure, why don't ye go over yerself?

COLIN. On me tod?

CLARENCE. Yah!

COLIN *considers this*.

COLIN. Buzz off a few Rastafarians. (*Dublin accent*.) Rasta-fari! Dread-eye! Jah live!

CLARENCE *titters*.

D'ye like that, do ye? D'ye like that?

CLARENCE. Very good.

COLIN. You're comin' to Jamaica with me, so ye are.

CLARENCE. Ahhh…

COLIN. You're comin' to Jamaica with me, Clarence.

CLARENCE. Wouldn't be my cup of tea now, Colin.

COLIN. Why not?

CLARENCE. Too hot.

COLIN. Ahhh.

CLARENCE. Besides… they'd all think I was Santa Claus over there.

COLIN *starts laughing*.

COLIN. *You* are Santa Claus! What are ye gettin' me for Christmas this year, Santy?

CLARENCE *thinks about this*.

CLARENCE. A bag of soot!

COLIN (*infantile voice*). But I wasn't bold, Santy.

CLARENCE. That's not what my little elf spies told me.

COLIN *laughs*.

COLIN. What are ye gettin' Ray?

CLARENCE. Ohhhh.

CLARENCE *scratches his beard*.

COLIN. I know what ye can get Ray!!

CLARENCE. What?

COLIN. A wig! Get 'im a red wig!

CLARENCE. Ah, now, Colin, Colin, Colin.

COLIN (*under his breath*). Fuck 'im.

Short pause.

CLARENCE. Do yez fight a lot, do yez?

COLIN. The odd time, yeah.

CLARENCE. Aw, yez shouldn't be fighin' now. Yez shouldn't be fightin'.

COLIN. Hate fightin', do ye?

CLARENCE. Hate it.

Short pause.

COLIN. Bit of a pacifist?

CLARENCE. Sort of. (*Short pause*.) Mind you... whenever I see that *bastard* up the way...

COLIN. Who's this now?

CLARENCE. Ah, the local bigshot. Owns a hardware shop in the village.

COLIN. Businessman?!

CLARENCE. Suppose ya could call him that.

COLIN. Hate them businessmen.

CLARENCE. Half businessman, half farmer.

COLIN. Them and the bankers! Fuckin' destroyed the world, they have.

Short pause.

CLARENCE. This fella now destroyed my dog.

COLIN. Destroyed yer dog?

CLARENCE. Had 'im put down.

COLIN. He had yer dog put down?

CLARENCE *nods yes.*

CLARENCE. Gave 'im a small bite on the leg, that's all.

COLIN. That all?!

CLARENCE. That's all! Shot up the arse! That's all the bastard needed. Not even a stitch.

COLIN. Shotgun up the arse! That's what he should of got. Fuckin'...

Enter RAY, *putting a nipped cigarette back into the box.*

D'ye hear this, Ray?

RAY *remains standing behind his seat.*

RAY (*very aggressive*). Wha'?!

COLIN. Some businessman fuckhead had his dog put down. Dog didn't do fuck-all to 'im either. Tell 'im, Clarence. Tell 'im. Gave 'im a little bite on the leg, that's all. Fucker didn't even need a stitch.

CLARENCE. Shot up the arse. That's all he needed.

COLIN. Shotgun up the arse! Fuckin'… dirt bird.

Short pause.

RAY. That doesn't sound righ' now, I have to say.

CLARENCE. No no no, sure… he pulled up the trouser of his… the leg of his trouser and… a blemish! That's all it was.

RAY *shakes his head and waves his hand.*

RAY (*slightly aggressive*). I'm sayin'… it's not righ' what he did.

COLIN. Fuckin' righ' it isn't! Should be punished for that! Should be made eat to elephant shit for two whole weeks and then kneecapped. All them businessmen and bankers! Destroyed the world!

COLIN *starts shaking his head.* RAY *gives him a dirty look and shakes his head.*

RAY. Type of dog was he?

CLARENCE. Springer.

RAY. Great dog.

CLARENCE. Aren't they?

COLIN. Fucker lives around here, Ray.

RAY (*to* CLARENCE). That righ'?

CLARENCE. Up the way. Lives in the second house just before the village. Always has the big black car outside.

RAY. D'ye want me to do a number on 'im? (*Smiles.*) Get 'im comin' out of house some nigh'…

CLARENCE. God no! God no!

RAY. Relax. I'm only kiddin' with ye.

RAY *sits.*

CLARENCE. I loved Doyle. But I didn't love 'im that much.

RAY (*amused*). That his name?

CLARENCE. 'Twas.

RAY. Gas name for a dog.

> CLARENCE *nods a couple of times.* CLARENCE *reaches for the bottle.*

CLARENCE. Named him after…

COLIN. That cunt has me blood boilin' now, so he does.

> RAY *rolls his eyes.*

Seriously though, Ray.

CLARENCE. Ah sure… he's been punished for his sins now, so he is.

COLIN. How?

CLARENCE. That… hardware shop of his is doing no business at all. Feck-all! Shutters will be coming down on it permanently.

COLIN. Still.

> RAY *dismisses him with a wave.*

RAY. Who d'ye name 'im after?

> COLIN *shakes his head. He picks up his flagon and uncaps.* CLARENCE *uncaps the whiskey bottle.*

CLARENCE. Doyle?

RAY. Yeah.

CLARENCE. Named him after a very good friend and colleague of mine. Connor Doyle.

> CLARENCE *pours whiskey into his cup.* COLIN *takes a slug from his flagon.*

Used to go over to his flat on the South Circular Road whenever there was a midterm break or one of those religious holidays…

RAY. Slaughtered?

CLARENCE. Isn't the word for it. Sure, on my third or fourth day in that flat I'd start seeing things coming out of the bloody walls.

CLARENCE *takes a sip of his drink.*

RAY. Hmmph. Any pink elephants?

CLARENCE. Never! Never saw a pink elephant. Plenty of rats and mice though. I swear to God, Ray... I used to see them scurrying by the whole time. '*You've rats, Doyle! I'm telling ya! You've rats!*'

RAY *laughs.*

Hmmph. Good ol' Doyle.

COLIN *puts his flagon down on the ground.* CLARENCE *smiles to himself. There follows several seconds of silence.*

Hell of a drinker.

RAY. Yeah?

CLARENCE. Aw, for God's sake. Two bottles of Huzzar for brunch. When he was drinking, that is. On and off it the whole time. Like myself. But when he was on it... (*Short pause.*) Yellow Man! That's what his students used to call 'im.

RAY *gives him a puzzled look.*

Went yellow from all the drink.

RAY *nods his head and wags his finger.*

RAY. Should of twigged that one.

CLARENCE. Jaundice.

RAY. Me own mother went that way.

CLARENCE. Ah, did she, poor woman.

COLIN. What about Ma?

RAY (*stressing*). Went yellow from the drink.

COLIN. Oh.

COLIN *blesses himself.*

RAY. Oul fella went red.

All of a sudden the Austrian wall clock behind COLIN *begins to chime.* COLIN *and* RAY *are a little bit startled, more so* COLIN. CLARENCE *is amused. He titters.* COLIN *is now looking over his shoulder at the clock. He turns his head back around and looks at* CLARENCE.

COLIN. Didn't know what that was.

The clock continues to chime. All in all it chimes eight times.

Pause.

RAY. Nice clock, that.

CLARENCE. Aw, she's a nice one alright.

Something occurs to COLIN.

Chimes every half hour as well. Just the once though.

COLIN. That's mad.

RAY. Wha'?!

Short pause.

COLIN. The thing start ringin'… just after you mentioned Ma and Da.

RAY. Where are ye goin' with this, Colin?

COLIN. I'm just sayin', like.

RAY. Sayin' wha'?!

COLIN. Ye know what I'm sayin'. The thing start…

RAY. The thing start ringin' because it's eight o'clock! Look! *Eight – o' – clock.*

CLARENCE. Austrian wall clock, that.

RAY *is still looking at* COLIN.

Been up there since I was a baby.

RAY. What was that?

CLARENCE. Been up there since I was a baby.

RAY. So you grew up here?

CLARENCE. I did.

Short pause.

RAY. Would that be an antique?

CLARENCE *hesitates.*

CLARENCE. Not at all. It's just old.

CLARENCE *takes a sip from his whiskey.* RAY *looks at the clock.*

RAY. Nice clock though.

CLARENCE. Ah, she is, yeah.

Short pause.

RAY. And she doesn't wake ye up in the middle of the night? All the ringin' and what have ye?

CLARENCE. Not at all.

RAY. Wake *me* up, it would.

CLARENCE. Bit of a light sleeper?

RAY *nods yes.*

RAY (*pointing at* COLIN). See him. Sleep through a bleedin' earthquake.

CLARENCE (*tittering*). Is that righ'?

A smiling COLIN *nods yes.*

Probably sleep through an earthquake myself.

RAY. Yeah?

CLARENCE. This stuff helps. (*Hoists up cup.*)

COLIN. Love yer whiskey, don't ye?

CLARENCE. Like a drop alright. (*Pause.*) Starting to slow down a bit now, the last few years. Doctor's orders!

Short pause.

RAY. That's the same with Pascal.

CLARENCE. Pascal?

RAY. The uncle.

CLARENCE. Oh. (*Winks to himself.*) Great name.

RAY. Used to horse the drink out of it, then he slowed down. And I don't mean to spook ye out here, Clarence, but that's when he got very sick. When he slowed down.

CLARENCE. Ow, happens. System is so used to it. Like anything else.

Short pause.

RAY. Tell you a story about Pascal.

CLARENCE. Great name that! Great name!

COLIN. Pascal had only one lung.

CLARENCE. Did he?

COLIN *nods yes.*

Sure, no wonder his health deteriorated.

RAY *goes to speak.*

John Wayne had only one lung. D'ye know what he said to the doctor...

RAY. Can I tell me story please?

CLARENCE. All ears!

CLARENCE *puts his cup down on the table.*

RAY. Pascal had a job out in the sticks somewhere. Swords... somewhere like that. Some granny's gaff.

COLIN. Love this story, I do!

RAY. He's in the kitchen, righ'? Tryna get the water back. Plumber!

CLARENCE. Right.

RAY. Starts complainin' about his tooth. (*Impersonating Pascal*.) 'Aw, me tooth, me tooth! Bleedin' killin' me.' The oul granny starts rootin' round lookin' for an aspirin or somethin' like that. Can't find any. Pascal asks her if she's any whiskey.

CLARENCE *titters*.

She tells him she does. Comes back a minute later with a bottle. A full bottle. (*Impersonates granny*.) '*Here ye go now, Pascal*.' Pascal's like... 'Just a drop now, just a drop.' So anyway... oul granny comes back into the kitchen a few minutes later... tells him that she's going to the shops, but that she'll leave the bottle with 'im just in case he needs another little drop for his tooth. Pascal's like... 'Eh... Okay, okay, just in case.' (*Short pause*.) Oul granny comes back about... half an hour, forty minutes later... no sign of Pascal, bottle's completely empty.

CLARENCE *burst out laughing*. COLIN *starts laughing as well*.

Polished it off in half an hour.

CLARENCE *continues to laugh*.

COLIN. Got her water back though.

RAY. Aw, she got her water back alrigh'. Best plumber in Ireland, Pascal.

CLARENCE *continues to laugh*.

Might be a huge drinker, but he was still a hell of a plumber!

CLARENCE. Aw, that's a great story, that is. Great story. (*Short pause*.) Aw lads, I tell ya, I'm glad I met yaz. Glad I met yaz. Glad I went over to the car that time. (*Takes a sip of his whiskey*.) The moon was glistening on the bonnet when I was walkin' over to yaz.

COLIN *looks at* RAY *in bafflement*. RAY *winks at him*.

RAY. We're probably gonna have to head off now in the next few minutes.

CLARENCE. Sure, what's the rush?

RAY *lifts up his flagon*.

RAY. Don't want to get too much of this into me. End up drivin' into a ditch. Worse still... killin' somebody.

CLARENCE. Aw... that's... that's... that's very responsible of ya, Ray.

RAY. Too much drink-drivin' on the road. (*Short pause*.) Feel a bit drunk as it is. (*Pause*.) We could always sleep in the car, I suppose. Pull the front seats back. (*Short pause*.) That would be uncomfortable though.

CLARENCE. Sure, yez can stay in the caravan.

Pause.

COLIN. Have a caravan, do ye? Have a caravan?

CLARENCE. I do.

RAY. Where is it?

CLARENCE. Out the back.

COLIN. Is it big, is it? Is it big?

CLARENCE. Wouldn't be one of the bigger ones now, but sure... there's a fold-out section in the middle where yez can lie down.

COLIN. Nice one.

CLARENCE. Throw yez a few blankets... couple of pillows.

RAY. Problem solved.

CLARENCE *nods*.

CLARENCE. Ah, this is great now. Great havin' a bit of company for the night. Only bit of company I get these days is Hubert Joe... down in McGuirk's.

COLIN (*amused*). Hubert Joe.

CLARENCE. Mmmmm. Only get six words out of him all night. Not joking with ya. Does be staring into his pint all night.

RAY. What's the story with the caravan?

CLARENCE *gives him a puzzled look.*

How long d'ye have it?

CLARENCE. 'Bout twenty years or so. Bought it off a Wexford man. Silliest purchase of my life, if I'm to be totally honest with yez, lads.

RAY. Why?

CLARENCE. Sure, I've only ever used it twice. And that was to sell books. Filled with all the books I bought over the years and… had a book sale in the village. Had another one in Glendalough. John Maguire ran me out there. Ran me back as well.

RAY. Make any money at all?

CLARENCE. Not at all. Sure, only sold half of them. Other half are still stacked down the back. So if you fancy a read in the morning, lads…

COLIN. Nah, yer alrigh'. He might though. Loves readin' books.

RAY. Give over, would ye. Last book I read was nearly three year ago.

CLARENCE. What was it?

Short pause.

RAY. *The Horse Whisperer.*

CLARENCE. Oh.

RAY. Found it on the 20B.

CLARENCE. Remember that bus. Didn't they make a film about that?

RAY *(half-smiling)*. The 20B?

CLARENCE *laughs.*

CLARENCE. The book.

RAY. They did, yeah. *(Pause.)* Any chance of havin' a look at this caravan, Clarence? Wouldn't mind havin' a peep at it.

CLARENCE. Come on so.

RAY gets up, as does CLARENCE. COLIN remains seated.

Might be a bit nippy out here tonight now, lads.

COLIN. Ah sure, we're use to that.

CLARENCE. What?

Short pause.

RAY. Talkin' about?

COLIN. Jokin'.

RAY shakes his head.

RAY. Here.

RAY puts his hand into his jeans pocket. CLARENCE looks concerned.

You can go down to the off-licence, so ye can. (*Takes out a couple of notes. He holds out a twenty-euro note.*) Flagon of Linden Village and a naggin of… what's that yer drinkin'? (*Looks at the bottle of whiskey.*) Paddy's. Naggin of Paddy's. (*Holding out the note for COLIN to take.*) Token of my appreciation for lettin' us stay in the caravan. Take the bleedin' money, will ye?

COLIN *slowly takes it.*

Come on, Clarence.

CLARENCE *doesn't move. He still looks concerned.*

Are ye alrigh', Clarence?

CLARENCE (*to COLIN*). What ye said there a second ago… about… being use to the cold.

COLIN. I was jokin', Clarence.

RAY. Always switchin' the heat off.

CLARENCE. What?

RAY. In the gaff. Always switchin' it off. Save a bit a money, ye know what I mean.

CLARENCE *gives a slow and unconvinced nod.*

Come on, Clarence. (*Puts his arm around* CLARENCE.)
Show us this caravan.

RAY *guides him out.* CLARENCE *stops.*

CLARENCE. Are you not comin' out, Colin?

RAY. He's goin' to the offo. Go to the bleedin' offo, you, will ye.

RAY *guides a concerned-looking* CLARENCE *out of the
room.* COLIN *looks at* RAY *scornfully as he guides*
CLARENCE *offstage. They exit stage right.*

Last caravan I was in was down in Wexford. Blackwater!
D'ye ever hear of there?

COLIN *shakes his head. He picks up his flagon.*

COLIN (*through gritted teeth*). Treatin' me like I'm fuckin'
Kevin. Treatin' me like I'm fuckin' Kevin! I'm not a fuckin'
slave!

COLIN *takes a large slug. The stage lights slowly start to
come down.*

Scene Three

The stage lights come up. CLARENCE *is standing, a cup of
whiskey in his hand.* RAY *is now sitting where* COLIN *had
been seated. His and* COLIN'*s flagons are on the log table. He
is holding one of* CLARENCE'*s daughter's paintings in both
hands. He is looking at* CLARENCE. *Aaron Copland's 'Lincoln
Portrait' is now playing. We hear the narrator's voice on the
record. It's a very grand American voice.*

CLARENCE *starts to speak the same words as the narrator. He
does this in almost perfect sequence and in his own voice.
Occasionally he overlaps the narrator.* CLARENCE *is now a
little bit drunk.*

CLARENCE.... 'As I would not be a slave, so I would not be a master. This expresses my idea of democracy! Whatever differs from this, to the extent of the difference, is no democracy!'

Instrumental section. RAY *winks at* CLARENCE.

There's more! Not done yet.

RAY. Okay.

Music.

CLARENCE *takes a quick sip of his whiskey. He continues the narration introducing the Gettysburg Address.*

Trumpets.

CLARENCE.... 'That from these honoured dead, we take increased devotion to that cause for which they gave their last full measure of devotion. That we here highly resolve, that this nation...'

Aw! skipped a bloody line.

NARRATOR. That this nation...

CLARENCE. 'Under God! Will have a new birth for freedom! And that government, of the people, by the people, and for the people, shall not perish from the earth!'

CLARENCE *drops his arms and bows his head.* RAY *puts down the painting and claps. The piece ends with a glorious crescendo.*

Ahh, I fucked up the end.

RAY. Ah, don't worry about it.

CLARENCE *shakes his head.*

CLARENCE. Whiskey must be kickin' in.

RAY. That's it. Relax yer bones.

CLARENCE *sits and groans.*

Tired?

CLARENCE. I could do it again.

RAY. Yer alrigh'. Once was enough.

Silence. CLARENCE *stretches out his legs.*

He was a tall oul bugger, Lincoln, wasn't he?

CLARENCE. He was. Had that gangly disease.

RAY. Made him mad skinny?

CLARENCE. And tall.

RAY. Die from it?

CLARENCE. No, sure... he was shot.

RAY. That's righ'!

CLARENCE. Assassinated.

RAY. Everyone bleedin' knows that. Even Colin probably knows that.

CLARENCE. Hmmph.

RAY *picks up the painting and looks at it.*

CLARENCE *pours himself another drop of whiskey.*

RAY. See you're in this, Clarence.

RAY *turns the painting around and points at a face in the painting.* CLARENCE *nods.*

CLARENCE. I'm in a fair few of them. Always a face in the background.

RAY. That a symbol for somethin'?

CLARENCE. Not enough in her life I suspect.

Silence.

RAY *continues to look at the painting.*

RAY. This is some heavy shit, Clarence.

CLARENCE. Mmmmm.

RAY. Nuclear bombs and crucifixes.

CLARENCE. Very influenced by Goya. That's her favourite.

RAY. Heard of 'im.

CLARENCE. Heard of a lot of people.

RAY. Mmmm. (*Still looking at the painting.*) Real... end-of-the-world painting.

CLARENCE *belches.*

CLARENCE. Sure, that's what it's called.

RAY. The End of the World?

CLARENCE. *End Days.*

RAY. So I'm on the button.

CLARENCE. You're on the button.

Short pause. RAY *looks at the painting one last time then leans it against the log.*

RAY. And is it?

CLARENCE. What?

RAY. The end of the world.

CLARENCE. Not at all. (*Short pause.*) That's just oul doomsayer talk. It's... it's... it's gonna take a lot more than an economic crisis to end this world.

RAY. Nuclear war?

CLARENCE. That's one way it could end.

RAY. Them bleedin' Iranians.

RAY *reaches for his flagon of cider.*

CLARENCE. Don't forget the North Koreans.

RAY. Mmmmm.

RAY *uncaps his cider.*

Colin's convinced it's the end.

CLARENCE *nods and smiles.*

Mind you, Colin's also convinced that there's aliens.

CLARENCE. Wouldn't rule it out.

RAY. Ah, Clarence.

CLARENCE. All ye need is a sun. And sure there's billions of
    them. You get a planet in close proximity… like us, for
    example!

RAY (*shaking head*). We're only a fluke.

CLARENCE. There could be billions of flukes.

> RAY *shakes his head.*

RAY. Not in my book.

> RAY *takes a swig from his cider.*

CLARENCE. Writing a book, are ya?

> RAY *smiles.*

> What's it about?

> *Pause.*

RAY. Colin.

> CLARENCE *starts tittering.* RAY *puts cap back on flagon
> and then rests it back down on the log.*

CLARENCE. That's what ya should do. Write a book about
    Colin. I'd say ya could do it.

RAY. Why d'ye think that?

CLARENCE. Ah, yer smart. And ya have a certain wit about
    ya. That thing ye said about the Samurais.

RAY. Sure, that was only one thing

CLARENCE. Ah, there was other stuff as well.

> *Pause.*

RAY. Wouldn't have time to write a book about the fucker
    anyway. Have to babysit 'im the whole time.

CLARENCE. Really?

> RAY *nods a couple of times.*

RAY. Retarded.

RAY smiles. CLARENCE grins back at him.

CLARENCE. Retarded?

RAY. Yeah. One of the borderline ones. (*Small laugh.*) Ah, he's just stupid, that's all.

RAY gives a small laugh.

Pause.

CLARENCE. But ya still have to look after him?

RAY thinks about this.

RAY. It's more of a case of lookin' out for him.

CLARENCE. Right. (*Short pause.*) And how long have ya been doing that for?

RAY. All me fuckin' life.

CLARENCE. Ah, Jesus.

RAY. Wha'?

CLARENCE. That's a long time, Ray.

RAY. What are ye gettin' at here, Clarence?

CLARENCE hesitates.

CLARENCE. Well… he's obviously holding ya back.

RAY. Holdin' me back?

CLARENCE. From doing other things. From getting on with yer life.

RAY. I am gettin' on with me life.

CLARENCE. Not if yer looking after Colin the whole time.

RAY. I'm not lookin'… (*He sighs. A short pause follows.*) He's not just me brother, Clarence. He's like… he's… me right arm.

CLARENCE. Your right arm?

RAY. He's me best mate. Been me best mate for... since I took 'im on at the window cleanin'. That's like... twelve year or somethin'.

CLARENCE. But that doesn't mean ya can't... I mean, ye might want to get married and have a family some day.

RAY. Don't know about that.

CLARENCE. Ah, I'm sure ya do now.

RAY. After what you told me about your marriage.

CLARENCE. Don't regret it. Not for one minute. Might of been a very turbulent marriage but... we did have some good times. And I do have two daughters.

Short pause.

RAY. Can't see it happenin', Clarence. But if it does! And I *very very* much doubt it... I'm still gonna look out for 'im.

CLARENCE. Of course! Of course! I'm not tellin' ya to abandon him or anything like that. I'm just saying... get out there and live your life.

RAY. Okay, Clarence.

CLARENCE *gives a nod. A short pause follows.*

What's keeping the fucker? He's probably waffling the ears off one of the natives.

CLARENCE. Aw, he's a character alrigh'.

RAY. The fuckin' stories I could tell ye about 'im. (*Pause.*) Filled out a FAS form one time before, righ'?

CLARENCE. Right.

RAY. Wanted to do a computer course, if ye can believe that.

CLARENCE. Huh.

RAY (*nodding his head and smiling*). Yeah. Anyway, instead of puttin' down male for sex, which is what anyone else would do. What does he put down? Fuckin' heterosexual.

CLARENCE *titters.*

I mean… why the fuck would FAS want to know what sexuality he was. (*Shakes his head.*) Sure, he wanted to go to Iraq to work on sites a couple of years ago. (*Colin's voice.*) 'Great money! Great money!' (*Own voice.*) 'Yeah, Colin, but we'll end up gettin' our heads blown off.' (*Colin's voice.*) 'No we won't! All we have to do is wear Irish jerseys!'

CLARENCE *starts tittering again.* RAY *shakes his head.*

I mean… have ye ever heard the likes. Thinks an Irish jersey is gonna stop a mad Iraqi from killin' ye. (*Short pause.*) Sure, just there yesterday in Blessington he wanted to put ten euro on a horse that was sixty-five to one. Only reason why he wanted to put money on the horse was because he liked the name. Vietnam!

CLARENCE. Yaz were in Blessington yesterday?

RAY. Eh… just… floatin' round, ye know.

CLARENCE *nods his head a couple of times. He seems a little bit doubtful about what* RAY *has just said.*

What would ye be up to if we weren't here, Clarence.

CLARENCE. Eh… watching telly in the bedroom I suppose.

RAY *nods a couple of times. Pause.*

You's are in a bit of trouble, aren't yaz?

RAY *sighs.*

RAY. Like I said to ye in the caravan, Clarence… (*Sighs again.*) We're not in any trouble, Clarence. Honest!

Short pause.

CLARENCE. So yaz aren't on the run, or anything like that?

RAY *starts laughing.*

RAY. No.

CLARENCE. So…

Short pause. RAY *looks uncomfortable.*

You's are out of home. That's what it is, isn't it.

RAY *hesitates*.

RAY (*weakly*). No.

CLARENCE. No shame if yaz are. Was homeless myself for a few days. Wife wouldn't let me into the house. Was on one of my mad benders.

RAY *gives an unconvincing shake of his head*.

RAY. We're not out of home, Clarence.

CLARENCE. Honestly now? Because... the way yaz ate that chicken and and and... the old beards and... I'll still let yaz stay in the caravan for the night. (*Short pause.*) Yaz are out of home, aren't yaz?

Short pause.

RAY. We are, yeah. No point lyin' to ye. (*Short pause.*) Put out of our own home, so we were.

CLARENCE. Why?

RAY. That's the thing. Done absolutely nuttin' wrong.

CLARENCE. So why were yaz put out? Who put yaz out?

RAY. Thomas. The brother we were talkin' about earlier. Came back from England and fucked us out of the gaff. Threatened us with a knife! Big mad carvin' knife! Told us if we didn't leave the gaff he'd cut us up.

CLARENCE. Jesus.

RAY. That's the type of person he is. Fuckin' scumbag! Remember what Colin said about him? All true. Thinks he's a fuckin' gangster, so he does. Hmmmph! Got his come-uppin's from a gangster. Last summer, righ'?

CLARENCE. Right.

RAY. Some young fella was dealin' on Thomas's patch. *Oh!* I forgot to mention. Thomas is a drug dealer. Deals drugs to young people.

CLARENCE. Righ'.

RAY. So this young fella who's dealin' on Thomas's patch...
Thomas finds out about it. Gives the young fella the slaps.
Turns out... this young fella is the cousin of one of the
biggest gangsters in North Inner City Dublin, '*The Duck*'! (*A
beat*.) Soon as Thomas finds this out... *ppphheeew*! Packs a
bag and goes to England. That very day as well!

Short pause.

CLARENCE. But why did he put yaz out? I mean...

RAY. Doesn't like us, Clarence. Thinks we're wankers.

CLARENCE. Why though? I mean... did yaz do somethin'
tha'...

RAY. Done nuttin', Clarence. The fucker just doesn't like us.
Never has.

Pause.

CLARENCE. But sure... yez would of lived with him for years.

RAY *hesitates again*.

RAY. Came back from England all crazy, Clarence. Psyched to
bits. Must of been whackin' the drugs out of it over there. It
was the drugs!! The drugs had his head in a pickle. All that
coke. (*Short pause*.) Plus, he doesn't like us.

CLARENCE. Why though? I mean... ya can't just hate
someone for no reason.

RAY. Ah, but that's the thing. That's the thing. Ye see...
Thomas doesn't like the fact that me and Col have a very
strong bond. As you already know. (*Shakes his head*.) And
Thomas hates that! (*A beat*.) Thomas doesn't hang around
with Ray and Col. Thomas doesn't drink with Ray and Col.
(*Really stressing*.) Thomas doesn't clean the windows with
Ray and Col. Now that really melts his head. Took Colin
under me wing, but not him.

CLARENCE. And why didn't ye?

RAY. Can't be trusted. Sure, I'd bring him out with me and he'd
end up fleecin' a gaff. That's what he's like, Clarence. Bad to
the bone.

CLARENCE. Doesn't sound like a particularly desirable person now, I have to say.

RAY. Hmmph. That's puttin' it very very nicely. (*Pause*.) Poor Kevin. That's who I feel sorry for.

CLARENCE. That another brother?

RAY *nods yes*.

RAY. Baby of the family. Lovely lad.

Short pause.

CLARENCE. He didn't kick him out?

RAY. Doesn't have a problem with 'im. (*Short pause*.) But I guarantee ye, he's usin' 'im! He's usin' Kevin! Makin' 'im go to the shops and all that sort of stuff. (*Thomas's voice*.) '*Aw here, Kevin, go over to Martin's and get us a six-pack of Miller. Aw here, Kevin, go over to Kebab Club and get us a burger. Aw here, Kevin, go down to Nellie's and get us twenty John Player Blue.*'

RAY *looks at* CLARENCE *and shakes his head*.

Fucker's probably takin' his dole money off 'im. Never took one cent off 'im, Clarence! Could of had me hand out every week… (*Slaps the palm of his hand*.) '*Come on, Kevin. Pay up. Ye have to pay somethin'. Meself and Colin are payin' the bills.*' Never took one cent off 'im. (*Short pause*.) Very good to that young fella, I was.

CLARENCE. Report him to the Gards.

RAY. Sure, they'd do nuttin'. They'd just laugh at us. Tell us to go back and live in the gaff.

CLARENCE *starts shaking his head*.

CLARENCE. Ah, no no no no. Ya can't have your little baby brother living in that house. Not in that environment.

RAY. Soon as we get a pad for ourselves we'll let 'im live with us.

CLARENCE. Buts… (*Sighs*.) It's… it's… it's… It's you three that should be living in the house! Not him!

RAY. I know, I know. It's not righ'. (*Short pause*.) I mean, there I was... makin' the dinner every day. (*A slight smile creeps over his face*.) Cleanin' the gaff every day... Coz... Colin and Kev are incapable of doin' stuff like that. And then what happens? That fuckbag comes back from England, and fucks me out of me own gaff! (*Shakes his head*.) Fuckin' embarrassin'. Eight years younger than me, so he is. Laughin' stock of East Wall. Coz that fucker's probably goin' round tellin' loads of people he kicked us out. (*Pause*.) Hope Gramby gets that apartment studio for us. Says he'll have a word with the landlord. Only one-oh-five a week. Accepts rent allowance. (*Stressing*.) Won't be free for another couple of weeks though.

CLARENCE. A couple of weeks...

RAY. Gramby says there's a good chance we'll get it.

Long pause.

CLARENCE. Yaz can stay in the caravan until yaz get that place so.

RAY. Really?

CLARENCE. Might as well.

RAY *winks to himself. He stands up and walks over to* CLARENCE. *He puts out his hand for* CLARENCE *to shake*. CLARENCE *shakes it*.

RAY. Gentleman.

RAY *returns to his seat and sits. He reaches for his flagon and uncaps. The whole time smiling*.

We won't be a nuisance now. Won't see us in here at all.

CLARENCE. Ah sure, yaz can come in the odd time. Cup of tea and a sandwich. Few drinks at the weekend.

RAY *nods and smiles at him. He then puts the flagon up to his mouth*.

Yaz can be my sons for the next two weeks.

RAY. We'll be yer sons!

CLARENCE. Good, good. I'd like that. I'd like that very much.

RAY *takes a slug of his cider.*

Just do me one favour though.

RAY. Anythin' at all.

CLARENCE. Don't be fighting.

RAY. We won't be fightin'. Promise ye. (*Caps flagon.*) But seriously, Clarence… (*Rests flagon back down on log.*) That's not a favour. (*A beat.*) What can we do for ye? D'ye need this place painted or somethin'?

CLARENCE *titters.*

CLARENCE. Does it look like it could do with a bit of a paint-job?

RAY. No, I just… I'm just tryna find somethin' we can do for ye.

CLARENCE. Don't have to do anything. Just… don't be fighting.

Pause.

RAY *looks at the paintings.*

RAY. What about these? (*Picks painting up.*) Have a load of these, don't ye? Meself and Col could flog them off for ye. Sell them to a few of our customers. I'm actually on talkin' terms with a lot of them.

CLARENCE. Ah, no no. That won't be necessary.

RAY. Could make a rake of money for ye. Now I don't know the prices of artwork, but sure… you could put yer own estimate on it.

CLARENCE (*shakes his head no*). Rather hang on to them, Ray. I'll think of somethin'.

Pause.

CLARENCE *has a look at the back wall.*

RAY. Where the fuck is this clown? (*Shakes his head.*)

CLARENCE *smiles. After a few seconds his whole face lights up.*

CLARENCE. That's what ya can do for me.

RAY. Wha'?

CLARENCE. Ya can write about Colin.

RAY. Ahh, Clarence…

CLARENCE. No, no. That's what you're going to do for me.

Short pause.

RAY. Ye want me to write a book about Colin?

CLARENCE *titters.*

CLARENCE. Not a book, no. Wouldn't expect that of ya. (*Short pause.*) A short story. Three thousand words on your brother Colin.

RAY. What's that?

CLARENCE. What?

RAY. Three thousand words? How long is that?

CLARENCE. Oh, it's about… eight foolscap pages.

RAY. And how am I supposed to write three thousand words on Colin when Colin's gonna be sittin' in that bleedin' caravan with me? Seriously.

CLARENCE. Sure, ya can come in here and write it. And I'm sure there will be days when Colin will want to go for a walk or something.

RAY *gives a laugh of desperation and shakes his head.*

I'll give ya a hand with it if ya ever get stuck. We can go through it together…

RAY. Tryna to get me up the top of the classroom, are ye?

CLARENCE *purses his lips and bends his head down slightly. There follows a short pause.*

Let me have a think about it, Clarence. It's just… I haven't written anything since I was a bleedin' kid.

CLARENCE. Guarantee ya… soon as you start writing it, ya won't be able to stop.

RAY. Don't know about that.

COLIN (*offstage*). Big ole piece a cake!

CLARENCE. There's yer subject now.

RAY *gets up off his seat.*

RAY. I'll get that.

RAY *answers the door. Enter* COLIN *holding an off-licence bag. He is followed by* RAY. COLIN *is out of breath.* RAY *is eyeing him suspiciously.*

COLIN. Alrigh', homes.

CLARENCE. You're out of breath?

COLIN *nods and gives him a mad smile.* RAY *goes over to where he was sitting in the first two scenes, scooping his flagon off the table along the way.*

COLIN. Jogged back.

COLIN *pulls out a naggin of whiskey from the bag.*

For you!

He hands the naggin to CLARENCE. *He then pulls out a flagon.*

And for you.

COLIN *hands the flagon to* RAY.

CLARENCE. Really appreciate this, lads.

RAY (*indignantly*). I was the one who bought it for ye.

COLIN. And I was the one who got it! Anyway! I've an even better present than that for ye, Clarence.

CLARENCE. That righ'?

COLIN. You drunk, Clarence?

CLARENCE. Gettin' there.

COLIN. Shouldn't drink so much. It's bad for ye.

COLIN *lets out a big moronic laugh.* RAY *shakes his head.* COLIN *pulls out another flagon letting the bag drop to the ground. He sits, placing the new flagon down on the table and picking up the original one.* CLARENCE *places the naggin down on the log table.*

CLARENCE. So what's this present ya have for me?

COLIN. Patience, Clarence, patience.

COLIN *uncaps and takes a slug, as does* RAY. RAY *caps his flagon and then puts it down on the ground.*

CLARENCE. Ray here is going to write a novella about ya.

COLIN. A wha'?

CLARENCE. A novella.

COLIN. What's that?

CLARENCE. A short novel.

COLIN *is shocked.* RAY*'s jaw drops.*

COLIN. You're gonna write a novel about me?

RAY. You told me a short story, Clarence.

COLIN. Ah, no no no. Write a novel about me. Don't write a short story about me. Write a novel about me. That'd be a hundred times better, so it would!

RAY. Clarence.

CLARENCE. Way too hard of a task for him, Colin.

COLIN. But a novel would be better!

CLARENCE *titters.*

Seriously, Clarence.

CLARENCE. Sure, he might develop it into a novel.

RAY. I don't think I'll be able to write this short story, let alone a bleedin' novel.

CLARENCE. Ah, of course ya will. Nothing to ya! I'll supply the pen and paper by the way. Have a nice gold pen in there ya can use.

RAY. Ye wouldn't just supply me with a bucket of paint and a brush.

CLARENCE. Colin's gettin' the bucket of paint and brush.

RAY *rolls his eyes*. COLIN *is now looking at* CLARENCE.

You're gonna paint this room, so ye are. And sure, ya might as well paint the bench outside.

COLIN *has a big moronic smile on his face*.

COLIN. When d'ye want me to do this for ye?

CLARENCE. Any time ya like. But make sure ya get it done before yez leave.

COLIN. Tomorrow, like?

RAY. Clarence is lettin' us stay in the caravan until Gramby gets us that flat.

COLIN*'s jaw drops*.

I told 'im our situation, how we were kicked out of our gaff by that scumbucket and for no good reason.

COLIN (*to* CLARENCE). Scumbucket!

CLARENCE. So I heard.

Short pause.

COLIN. So yer lettin' us stay in the caravan?

RAY. Only until Gramby gets us that flat!

COLIN *looks at* CLARENCE *and shakes his head*.

COLIN. I think you might be an angel, Clarence. I really think you might be an angel.

CLARENCE. A pot-bellied angel.

COLIN. Huh. (*Pause.*) Santa Claus!! That's who ye are!

RAY *sniggers*.

That's who he is!

COLIN *takes another quick slug, caps, and then puts flagon down on the ground. He belches.*

CLARENCE. Bless ye.

COLIN *nods at him.*

RAY. We're gonna be Clarence's sons, so we are.

COLIN. We'll be yer sons alrigh'.

CLARENCE. Good.

COLIN. We'll be yer sons.

Short pause.

CLARENCE. All my life I've wanted a son, and now here I am with two of them. I'll drink to that.

CLARENCE *puts up his cup. He then takes a drink.*

COLIN. What colour d'ye want me to paint the room, Da? Paint it yellow, will I? Love bleedin' yellow! Look! (*Pointing at his runners.*) Look! (*He then points at his jacket.*) Look! Favourite colour, yellow.

CLARENCE. Ye can paint it yellow so. But... not the... not the bench. Ya can paint that black.

COLIN. Paint it black so.

RAY. He'll make a balls of it, Clarence.

COLIN. Won't make a balls of it! (*Short pause.*) Aw man, this is mad. An hour ago I'd bleedin' nuttin'! Livin' in a fuckin' car! Now I've a place to stay! A job! And me brother's writin' a fuckin' novel about me!!

RAY *rolls his eyes and shakes his head.* COLIN *picks up his flagon.*

The world has turned for Colin Cullen! (*Smiles to himself.*) Here! I've something to tell you, Clarence. I've something to tell you.

CLARENCE. Right. Where's this present you were telling me about?

COLIN. This is it!

CLARENCE (*baffled*). What?

Short pause.

COLIN. Yer gonna love this, so ye are. Yer gonna love this! (*Short pause.*) That bollix that had yer dog put down... won't be drivin' anywhere for a while. (*Moronic laugh.*) Slashed all his tyres, so I did. All four of them! Even done a shit on the bonnet! (*Moronic laugh.*) Wha'?

Short pause.

CLARENCE. Ye didn't do that, did ye?

COLIN. I did, yeah.

CLARENCE. Jesus, Mary and Joseph.

COLIN. Are ye not happy, are ye not?

RAY. I hope this is some sort of a joke, Colin.

Short pause.

COLIN. No.

RAY. Ye slashed his tyres?!

COLIN *nods his head a couple of times.*

Whatcha slash them with? Ye didn't slash his tyres.

COLIN. I did!

RAY. Whatcha slash them with then?

COLIN. This! (*Pulling the knife out of his tracksuit top.*)

RAY*'s face drops.* CLARENCE *puts his hands on his head.*

CLARENCE. Aw! Aw!

RAY. You fuckin' retard! You absolute fuckin' retard!

CLARENCE (*taking hands down*). Why did ye go and do that, Colin? Why did ye go and do that?

COLIN. Ye know why! Fucker put yer dog down!

CLARENCE. Eight years ago! Eight bloody years ago!

> COLIN *stares at him with a moronic look on his face.*

COLIN. Doesn't matter. (*Waving the knife.*) Shouldn't of done that. Shouldn't of have done that. Likes of that fucker that's destroyed the world. (*Slams the knife down on the table.*)

CLARENCE. Awww.

> CLARENCE *puts a hand on his forehead and sighs.* RAY *is now staring angrily at* COLIN.

COLIN (*to* CLARENCE). Wha'?! Wha'?! After doin' ye a bleedin' favour. Should be happy.

CLARENCE. Happy?!

COLIN. Yeah.

CLARENCE. Happy?! (*Short pause.*) The bastard's gonna be down here first thing in the morning with the Gards.

COLIN. No he won't.

CLARENCE. Of course he will. He'll suspect me straightaway.

COLIN. How?

CLARENCE. We have a history.

COLIN. Wha'?

RAY. They have a history! They don't like each other!

> *A very shook-up* CLARENCE *pours himself a large whiskey.*

That's righ', Clarence, get a whiskey into ye. Calm ye down. (*To* COLIN.) Fuckin' retard.

> COLIN *stares at* RAY. CLARENCE *knocks back his fresh whiskey.*

Good man. And don't worry about a thing, by the way. He's takin' the rap for this.

COLIN. Wha'?

RAY. You're takin' the rap for this.

COLIN. Uh... uh... I can't.

RAY. No option.

COLIN. Uh... uh... I... I'll end up back in the Joy [*a prison*].

CLARENCE *gives* COLIN *a worried look*.

RAY. *He* was in the Joy. I wasn't in the Joy.

COLIN. We have to go, Ray, seriously. We have to go!

RAY. Pppph. Not goin' anywhere. Stayin' in that caravan, I am. That righ', Clarence?

COLIN. B... b... bu'... bu'...

RAY. But nuttin'. You're takin' the rap for this and that's all there is to it. Sick of lookin' after ye, so I am. Fuckin' sick of it! Lookin' after ye all me life, ye fuckin' retard.

COLIN *gives* RAY *a hurtful look. He looks away and shakes his head.*

Short pause.

COLIN. Ye don't know what that place is like, Ray.

RAY. Best place for ye if ye ask me. Fuckin' retard.

COLIN. Stop callin' me that, Ray.

RAY. That's what ye are though. (*Leaning over and saying it directly to him.*) *A FUCKING REEEETAAARD!*

COLIN *picks up the knife and goes for* RAY *with it. He presses a knee into* RAY*'s chest and points the knife at* RAY*'s neck.* CLARENCE *is petrified.*

COLIN. Say that again! Say that one more time! Go on! Call me a retard!

CLARENCE. C... C... Colin!

COLIN. Call me a retard!

CLARENCE. Colin, please.

COLIN *keeps the knife against* RAY*'s throat for several seconds.* CLARENCE *is petrified.* COLIN *slowly moves away with the knife, staring at* RAY *with a crazy look in his eyes. He then moves for* RAY *again.* RAY *flinches.* CLARENCE *gasps.* CLARENCE *has become short of breath.* COLIN *whips off* RAY*'s hat with his free hand and steps back. We see* RAY*'s hair for the first time. It's a crop-style haircut, thick at the back and sides and thin on top. He has a fringe that comes halfway down his forehead. His hair is red.* CLARENCE*'s breathing has become very laboured.*

COLIN. Look at his hair, Clarence! Look at his hair! Fuckin' state of it! Look at it! Bleeding arangatang [*orang-utan*] fringe! That's what it looks like, doesn't it? An arangatang's fringe.

An embarrassed-looking RAY *starts shaking his head.*

Shave it off, Ray. Seriously. Shave it off. Not doin' yerself any favours. Won't have to wear this all the time.

COLIN *sniffs the hat.*

CLARENCE. Will ya... will ya put down the knife, Colin, please.

COLIN. Fuckin' bang off it! Going into the fire, this is.

RAY *grits his teeth and starts shaking his head.* COLIN *walks to the stove.*

RAY (*firmly*). Colin!

COLIN. No no. Goin' into the fire.

COLIN *puts the knife on top of the stove and opens the stove door.*

Watchin'? Are ye watchin'?

He throws the hat into the flames. He waves at the hat.

Bye-bye, smelly hat.

Slams the door shut and picks up the knife.

Look at 'im. He's bullin'.

Laughing, COLIN *walks back over to his seat.*

Doesn't have his wig any more. Huh. (*Remains standing by his seat.*) What's up, Clarence?!

CLARENCE. Ha… ha… h… h… have to be very… have to be very honest with ya, Colin…

COLIN. Wha'?

RAY. The man's petrified, so he is.

COLIN. You shut the fuck up! No one's talkin' to you! Are ye alrigh', Clarence?

CLARENCE *slowly shakes his head no. His breathing has worsened. He sits back in his chair.*

Have another sup of whiskey there for yerself.

CLARENCE. Ya… (*Heavy breaths. He points at the knife.*) Ya… ya not… ya not gonna do anything silly with that now, are ya?

COLIN. Might, yeah.

CLARENCE. Uh…

RAY. Relax, Clarence. He's not gonna do anythin' silly with the knife.

COLIN. Did I not tell you to shut the fuck up! Did I? Or did I not? (*Pause.*) I'll put the knife down if that's worryin' ye, okay?

CLARENCE *nods yes.* COLIN *slowly puts the knife down on the log.*

Knife is down.

He slowly sits, but sits in a way where he has a full view of RAY *and* CLARENCE.

Like meself.

CLARENCE *nods.*

Knife down.

CLARENCE (*gaspy*). Good lad.

COLIN (*looking at* RAY). Not too far though.

He winks at RAY *and then looks at* CLARENCE. *Short pause.*

Big ole piece of cake! (*Short pause.*) Not funny any more, sure it's not? No. Fuckin' scumbag now.

CLARENCE. Not a scumbag.

COLIN. Am a scumbag. (*Pointing at* RAY.) Him as well. (*Pause.*) Ye wanna know why we were kicked out of our gaff, Clarence? The real reason now.

RAY *shakes his head.*

Meself and *baldy* over there were makin' a skivvy out of our younger brother Kevin. (*Nods his head a couple of times.*) Makin' 'im do all types of shit. Makin 'im go to the offo! Makin' 'im go to the shops! We were even makin' 'im cook the dinner!

RAY. To give 'im somethin' to do.

COLIN. Aw, that's what ye used to say to 'im alrigh'.

RAY. Wasn't doin' anythin', Clarence. Sittin' on his arse all day, so he was. Daydreamin'.

COLIN. We only made 'im do them things coz we didn't want to do them for ourselves!!

RAY. No.

COLIN. Yes!! Fuckin' yes!! And! And! (*Brings it down a couple of notches.*) He didn't like 'im!

RAY. Aw, would ye stop, would ye.

COLIN. Ye didn't though! Fuckin' hated the young fella!

RAY. I hated me own brother.

COLIN. Fuckin' righ' ye did! And ye know why, Clarence? Ye know why? Coz little Kevin never looked up to 'im. (*Pointing at* RAY.) Looked up to Thomas though. Loved Thomas! Aww, that kid thought Tomo was a god. What are ye shakin' yer head for? Ye know it's the truth. He never looked up to ye! And that shouldn't of been, like! Coz you're the oldest, like! You were the one he should of looked up to.

RAY *continues to shake his head.*

Might of been the oldest, but ye certainly weren't the toughest. No. Tomo was the toughest. (*To* CLARENCE.) That's why he looked up to Tomo. And that drives 'im mad, so it does.

RAY. I don't know what to say.

COLIN. Say nothing! Say – fucking – nothing!

Pause.

CLARENCE*'s breathing improves. He is now breathing a little bit slower.*

CLARENCE. I don't know what exactly was going on in that house…

COLIN. Just after tellin' ye!

CLARENCE. Yes, I know, I know, bu'… (*A deep breath.*) There was… there was obviously some sort of power struggle going on and…

COLIN. Power trip, more like it! Soon as Thomas went to England, boom! Fuckin' baldy over there puts his foot down. Never put yer foot down when Thomas was in the house though, did ye? You weren't the master of the house then, were ya? Fucking slavedriver.

Short pause.

CLARENCE. This is what happens. Jesus… I could give yaz… so many examples in history…

COLIN. I don't want another history lesson, okay! No more history lessons! We're not yer students, okay! We're not yer fuckin' sons either!

CLARENCE. Okay okay okay okay.

CLARENCE *starts gasping again. And remains so for the duration of the piece.*

Short pause.

COLIN (*softly*). We're bad people, Clarence. Very bad people.

Short pause.

CLARENCE. Well then, that makes three of us.

COLIN. Wha'?!

CLARENCE. I'm a bad person too.

COLIN *stares at him.*

COLIN. How the fuck are you a bad person? You're not a bad person! You're after bringin' us into yer home. Yer after givin' us food and drink...

CLARENCE. Ah sure... anybody could of done that.

COLIN. No! Not anyone could of done that.

CLARENCE. I used to hit my wife, Colin.

COLIN. She never gave ye a son.

CLARENCE. Because I was hittin' her! (*Deep breath.*) I'd come in... with the few drinks down me and... I'd start pushin' her around. (*Another deep breath. His breathing has slowed down again.*) Sure, one time... (*Another deep breath.*) I pulled one of her earrings right out of her ear! Ripped it right out of her ear! All she did was ignore me. (*Deep breath.*) Spent the whole night in the A&E with the blood pourin' out of her – (*Deep breath.*) and there I was, sittin' in the back room the whole night... pourin' the drink into me. (*Deep breath.*) Now is that a nice person now, Colin?

Short pause.

COLIN. Yeah well... I betcha ye never locked 'er in the cupboard! That's what we used to do! Used to lock Kevin in · the cupboard whenever he didn't do somethin' that we wanted him to do.

RAY. To put the clampers on 'im! So he would do them things! And besides, we only put 'im in the cupboard twice.

COLIN. So that made it righ', did it? That made it righ'?!

RAY. Relax, would ye, Colin.

COLIN. No, I won't fuckin' relax! I'm in charge now! So you don't fuckin' tell me what to do! Doin' that all yer life, so ye have. That's coz I'm stupid, isn't it? 'Colin's stupid. Colin should be in the zoo.' That's what ye used to say when we were kids.

COLIN *notices* RAY *grinning*.

What are ye laughin' at? I'll come over there now and stick this in yer troth!

CLARENCE. Aw Jesus.

COLIN. Aw Jesus nuttin!! He's a fuckin' slither. He deserves to have this stuck in him.

CLARENCE *at this stage is petrified. He is once again short of breath.*

RAY. This is exactly the way Thomas was goin' on before he kicked us out. Remember? With the knife?

COLIN. I don't care! I don't fuckin' care!! We deserved to be kicked out! Fuckin' scumbags!

CLARENCE (*gaspy*). Yaz aren't.

COLIN *turns and faces* CLARENCE.

COLIN. Well then, what are we?

CLARENCE. Yaz… yaz…

COLIN. Speak!

CLARENCE. Yaz are decent.

COLIN. Ah, would ye fuck off, would ye!! (*Moving closer to* CLARENCE, *pointing the knife at him.*) We've robbed houses, Clarence! A window was open, a back door was open, boom! In we'd go and fleece the gaff! That's why I was in jail!! For fleecin' a gaff! Sure, we were gonna fleece yer fuckin' caravan, ye know that? His idea of course! Fuckin' slither! (*Stares at* RAY.) See him! See him! Hasn't had a proper friend in years, so he hasn't! Last friend he had was Jay Kelly. And that was like twenty year ago or some-thin'! Only reason why he's anythin' to do with me is coz I do the windows with 'im! And coz I'm the only one that'll put up with his bollocks. Isn't that righ'?!

COLIN *looks away and starts shaking his head.* RAY *secretly reaches down for his uncapped flagon.*

So are ye still gonna let us stay in yer caravan?! Are ye still gonna let us stay in yer caravan!! Are ye?!

CLARENCE *clutches his left arm and starts groaning.*

Fuck are ye playin' at?!

RAY *hurls his flagon off the side of* COLIN*'s head.* COLIN *stumbles back from the impact but doesn't fall. The knife comes out of his hand and lands several feet away from him. It lands near the exit to the kitchen.* RAY *runs towards* COLIN *and grabs him. He then punches him in the head. He pulls his head down and does it again.* COLIN *breaks away and runs to the front door.* RAY *runs after him. He catches* COLIN *at the front door. They are now both offstage so they can only be heard.* CLARENCE *is still clutching his left arm.*

CLARENCE (*faintly*). Not now. Please. Not now.

We hear RAY *thumping* COLIN.

RAY (*offstage*). Threatenin' yer own brother with a knife!

CLARENCE. Aw!

RAY (*offstage*). Yer own brother!

More blows from RAY *and squealing from* COLIN.

CLARENCE. Aine!

COLIN (*offstage*). I'm sorry! I'm sorry!

CLARENCE. I love ye, Aine. I love...

CLARENCE *groans again. The pain is immense. Sweat is dripping from his forehead.* CLARENCE *looks straight ahead, still clutching his left arm.*

13... 1315... Battle of... Battle of Carrickfergus. 1316...

We hear RAY *outside breathing heavily.* CLARENCE *groans again.*

Aw Jesus. Aw Jesus. (*Deep breath.*) Aine. (*Groans.*)

RAY (*offstage*). Fuckin' prick ye.

CLARENCE. Aine...

CLARENCE *gives a series of short sporadic groans, this time clutching his chest. After several seconds he slumps down on the chair, his arm hanging down over the side. Silence for several seconds.*

RAY (*offstage*). Look at ye! Whimperin' on the ground like a wuss. Ye alrigh' in there, Clarence? Any wonder at all ye scarpered that nigh' on Parnell Street?! Any wonder at all?! Left me on me tod to fight a load of muppets! Got the head lumped off me. (*Short pause.*) Only hard when there's a knife in yer hand.

After a few seconds, RAY *walks into the room. He sees* CLARENCE *slumped on the chair, eyes closed. He walks towards him.*

Clarence! Clarence! (*Shakes his arm.*) Clarence!

CLARENCE*'s head drops.* RAY *steps back in shock.*

Aw fuck.

Enter a battered-looking COLIN.

COLIN. Wha' is it?

RAY. *Fuck.*

COLIN. Wha' is it?!!

RAY *moves towards* CLARENCE. *He opens his mouth and puts his ear up to it.*

What's wrong with 'im? (*Short pause.*) What's wrong with 'im, Ray?

RAY. Shut up!! I'm tryna hear if he's breathin'.

COLIN. Aw, fuck.

Pause.

RAY. He's not breathin'.

RAY *takes his hand away.* CLARENCE*'s head drops again.*

COLIN (*putting his hands on his head*). Aw Jaysus.

Short pause.

RAY. Oul fella's after croakin' it.

Short pause.

COLIN. Aw Jaysus. (*Short pause.*) He's not dead.

RAY. He's dead, Colin.

COLIN. He's not he's not he's not. He… he… he… He's after faintin' or somethin'. (*Runs over to* CLARENCE.)

RAY. So why isn't he breathin' then?!

COLIN (*shaking* CLARENCE). Clarence! Clarence! Wake up, Clarence! Come on! Bleedin' wake up, will ye!

RAY *is now shaking his head.*

Clarence! Please! (*Shaking him again.*)

RAY. He's not gonna wake up, Colin! (*Short pause.*) He's dead!

COLIN *looks at* CLARENCE. *At this point he concedes to the fact that* CLARENCE *is indeed dead.*

Fuckin' killed 'im, ye did.

COLIN. Wha'?

RAY. That fuckin' crazy business with the knife! And slashin' yer man's tyres! Put a strain on his heart. Fuckin' killed 'im.

COLIN *slowly looks at* CLARENCE. *He sighs mournfully and kneels down before him.*

COLIN. Aw, Jaysus, Clarence. (*Almost on the verge of tears, he clasps* CLARENCE*'s hands.*) Jesus.

Silence for up to half a minute. RAY *is thinking.*

RAY. Did anyone see him gettin' in the car that time? Did they?!!

COLIN. I dunno!

> RAY *starts thinking again. He looks at the Austrian wall clock.*

I'm sorry, Clarence. I'm sorry. (*Crying.*) I'm really sorry.

RAY. Apologise to him again.

> COLIN *looks around at* RAY.

I'm serious! You apologise to that man again!

> COLIN *turns around and faces* CLARENCE.

COLIN. I'm sorry, Clarence. I'm really sorry.

RAY. And again!

> RAY *looks at the Austrian wall clock.*

COLIN. I'm sorry, Clarence. I'm really sorry.

> RAY *walks over to the clock.*

RAY. Did I tell ye to stop, did I?!

> RAY *puts his hands on the clock and starts shaking it.*

COLIN. I'm so sorry, Clarence.

RAY (*stepping back*). Fuck it.

> RAY *walks towards the kitchen. He spots the knife near the door and picks it up. He then exits into the kitchen.*

COLIN. I would never of... I wouldn't of gone crazy with the knife like that if... (*Whispers.*) Ray kept windin' me and... I was disappointed ye didn't like me present. I really thought it was a much better present than Ray's. (COLIN *looks up at* CLARENCE.) Aw Clarence.

> COLIN *drops his head onto* CLARENCE's *lap.* RAY *walks out of the kitchen holding one of* CLARENCE's *grocery bags.*

RAY. You keep apologisin' to him.

> COLIN *looks at* RAY *in disbelief.*

We have to eat, don't we?

COLIN *sighs*.

Exit RAY.

A few seconds later we hear the front door open. COLIN *looks at* CLARENCE. *He realises something. We hear a car door open.* COLIN *jumps up and starts pouring whiskey into* CLARENCE*'s cup. He then goes to put the cup into* CLARENCE*'s hand. Enter* RAY.

The fuck are ye doin'?!

COLIN. He wanted to die with a cup of whiskey in his hand.

RAY *glares at him. He then waves at him to move aside.* RAY *then takes the knife out of his tracksuit pocket, takes a hold of the blade with two fingers and then slides the handle along the palm of* CLARENCE*'s right hand. He then closes his hand around the handle.*

RAY. They'll think he done it.

COLIN. Done wha'?

RAY. Slash yer man's tyres, ye bleedin'…

Once again RAY *puts two fingers on the blade and then pulls it free from* CLARENCE*'s hand. He places the knife down on the table.*

Go on! Do yer thing! I'll make sure we're not leavin' anythin' behind.

RAY *starts looking at the table. He notices the cups.*

COLIN. What hand will I put it in?

RAY (*points at his right hand*). That hand!

COLIN *goes to put the cup into* CLARENCE*'s right hand. He stops.*

COLIN. Hold on! This'll take away his prints.

RAY. The prints are already on the handle!

RAY *shakes his head and picks up the two cups and the plate on the table. He exits into the kitchen with them.*

COLIN *carefully proceeds to put the cup of whiskey into* CLARENCE*'s hand, putting his thumb through the handle. He then props* CLARENCE*'s arm onto the arm of the chair.* COLIN *steps back and looks at him. Enter* RAY. *He too has a look.*

Bad idea.

COLIN. Wha'?

RAY *walks over and puts his two fingers on the rim of the cup and gently pulls it loose. He then gently places it down on the table.*

RAY. Get yer two flagons!

COLIN. He wanted to die with a cup of whiskey in his hand.

RAY. How the fuck's a cup supposed to stay in his hand after a heart attack?! (*Puts the cup on the table.*) Get yer two flagons.

A sulking COLIN *walks around to his chair and retrieves his two flagons.* RAY *starts looking for the flagon he struck* COLIN *with. He spots it close to the side of his chair. He picks it up and walks over to the seat he was sitting on.* COLIN *stands, holding his two flagons looking mournfully at* CLARENCE. RAY *puts the flagon down on the ground and grabs his jacket from the chair.* RAY *starts putting on his parka jacket.*

Some fuckin' tulip, you are. (*Zips up aggressively and then picks up both his flagons.*) We were in! We were fuckin' in! And you fucked it up! Would of let us stay out there for as long as we wanted. Wanted us to be his sons!

RAY *continues to stare at* COLIN *for several seconds, he then shakes his head and looks away.*

D'ye have everything now?

COLIN *nods yes.*

Do ye?! It's fuckin' important!

COLIN. I have everythin'.

RAY *stares at him for several seconds.*

Aw, Jesus, Ray, I feel fuckin' scaldy.

RAY. Yeah well, ye can feel scaldy in the car.

RAY *picks up his flagons and begins to exit.* COLIN *remains looking at* CLARENCE.

Are ye righ'?!

Short pause.

COLIN. Do *you* not feel scaldy at all?

RAY *glares at* COLIN.

RAY (*pointing at* CLARENCE). About this?

COLIN. Yeah! What else?

RAY. I'm not responsible for this.

COLIN. I know bu'… d'ye not feel scaldy at all?

RAY. Aw, I feel scaldy alrigh'. Very scaldy! But Colin, it's a different kinda scaldy. Not the scaldy you're feelin'.

Exit RAY.

COLIN. Aw Jaysus, Clarence. What have I done?

Pause.

Enter RAY.

RAY. Are ye fuckin' righ'?

COLIN *sits and puts his two flagons down on the ground in front of him.*

COLIN. Not goin'.

RAY. Wha'?!

COLIN. Stayin'.

RAY. Yer stayin'?!

A tearful COLIN *nods yes.*

Are ye out yer fuckin' mind, are ye? Ye heard what the oul codger said.

COLIN. Don't call 'im that!

RAY. *Okay! Okay! Okay!*

COLIN. Proper gentleman, so he was.

RAY. I know he was. Salt of the earth and what have ye. But ye do remember 'im sayin' that the pigs would be here in the mornin'? Ye do remember 'im sayin' that?

COLIN. Yeah.

RAY. So ye want to go back to jail?

COLIN *nods yes.*

Ye'll be done for manslaughter. That's like... eight year or somethin'.

COLIN. Six year.

RAY. Okay, six year!

COLIN. Should get twenty.

RAY *sighs.*

Pause.

RAY. He had a bad heart.

COLIN. Wha'?

RAY. The oul co... (*Stressing.*) He had a bad heart.

COLIN. How d'ye know?

Slight hesitation from RAY.

RAY. Told me. Told me when yer off down to the offo. (*Short pause.*) Now...

COLIN. And why didn't ye tell me that?!

RAY. Tellin' ye now.

COLIN. When I was goin' apeshit with the knife?!

RAY *shakes his head.*

RAY. Aw, Col.

COLIN. Seriously though, Ray.

     RAY *hesitates*.

RAY. I forgot! Too worried for meself. Really thought you were
     gonna stick me at one stage, Col.

     COLIN *starts shaking his head*.

COLIN. I wouldn't of stuck ye, Ray.

RAY. How was I supposed to know that?

COLIN. I wouldn't…

RAY. Mad fuckin' eyes on ye! Bulgin' out of yer head, so they
     were!

COLIN. Wha'?

RAY. You were like a man possessed, Colin. Like… like some
     sort of mad fuckin' werewolf.

COLIN. I wouldn't of stuck ye, Ray. Honest to Jesus. Ye have
     to believe me. There was no way…

RAY. Okay okay okay. Doesn't matter. Got ye back for that
     anyway.

COLIN. How?

RAY. Gave ye a few solids, didn't I?

COLIN. Deserve more than a few solids.

     RAY *rolls his eyes*.

RAY. Would ye of gone on like that if ye'd known he had a bad
     heart. Would ye have?

COLIN. No! Absolutely not.

RAY. Well, there ye go then. There is no way ye would of gone
     on like that if ye'd known he had a bad heart. No way! Coz
     yer a decent human bein', so ye are.

COLIN. Not a decent human bein'.

RAY. Yes you are. Yes you are. (*Smiling*.) Might of robbed the
     odd gaff alrigh', but deep down… yer a good oul skin.

COLIN *shakes his head and looks at* RAY.

Just keep thinkin' to yerself what I told ye.

COLIN. Wha' did ye tell me?

RAY *gets frustrated*.

RAY. *You wouldn't have gone apeshit if ye'd known he had a bad heart.* (*Short pause*.) You have to keep thinkin' that!

COLIN *drops his head*.

Don't worry, Col. Ye'll get over this, ye will.

COLIN. Never gonna get over this.

RAY *rolls his eyes again. A short pause follows*.

I... I... I... I could become a monk... an'... an'... an'... be a monk for years and I'd... still be fucked up over this.

RAY. They wouldn't accept ye.

COLIN. Wha'?

RAY. The monks. They wouldn't accept ye.

COLIN. They'd be righ'.

Short pause.

RAY. Look, Col...

RAY *crouches down beside* COLIN. *He puts his hand on his back*.

You will get over this. I promise ye.

COLIN *starts shaking his head*.

Ye will ye will ye will. Ye'll get over it. And I'll help ye get over it. I'll be here for ye! Like I've always been, righ'? Righ'?

COLIN *nods his head a couple of times*.

I was there for ye when you were in the Joy, and I'll be here for ye now. (*Short pause*.) Anyone else visit ye when ye were in the Joy?

COLIN *shakes his head no*.

RAY. Ma or Da even?

COLIN *shakes his head no.*

Just yer brother Ray. Yer righ' arm. (*Pause.*) Now this is what we're gonna do, Collie baby. We're gonna get in that car. We're gonna drive back to Dublin. Probably get back there before twelve. We're gonna drink our flagons in the piggery. And then tomorrow mornin'… we're gonna go round to Gramby's, and see what the story is with that bedsit. Alrigh'?

COLIN *doesn't respond.* RAY *pats him on the back and stands.*

Come on. I'll even let ye listen to Stevie Wonder all the way back in the car.

COLIN. Don' wanna listen to Stevie Wonder.

RAY *rolls his eyes.*

RAY. Well then, ye can drink yer flagon. (*Pause.*) Time to go, Colin.

Short pause.

COLIN. I'll be out in a minute.

RAY. Good lad. (*Starts to exit.*) Now don't take all day.

COLIN. I'll be out in a minute!!

RAY. Okay, okay, okay.

RAY *exits, rolling his eyes. A pause follows.* COLIN *looks at the corpse. He covers his face with his hands and sighs. After a few seconds he takes them away and sighs. He stands up abruptly. We hear the car engine being started up. We then hear the first few lines of Stevie Wonder's 'I Believe'.*

RAY *lowers the volume down.*

COLIN. Aw Jaysus. (*Short pause.*) If I had of known, Clarence. I swear to Jesus… if only bleedin'…

Looks away and sighs. A few seconds later he looks again at CLARENCE. *On the verge of tears again.*

You were such a nice man, so ye were. You were such a nice man. And I would of loved to have been yer son. Really! Never really had much of a father meself. He was alrigh' now, bu'… (*Sighs*.) Drink and sleep. That's what we used to call 'im.

COLIN *looks sorrowfully at* CLARENCE. *He slowly stands with his head down.*

Don't feel good about this, Clarence.

A pause follows. COLIN *looks at* CLARENCE, *bites down on his lip and looks away.*

Goodbye, Clarence.

COLIN *goes to exit. He knocks over his two flagons on the ground in front of him.*

Aw Jaysus.

COLIN *scoops up his two flagons and exits at a fast pace with his head down. We hear the front door shut. We hear a car door open and close. After a few seconds we hear the car reverse and then drive off. There is silence.* CLARENCE *slumped in his armchair. Silence for several seconds. All of a sudden the Austrian clock starts chiming. Nine chimes. Silence. The stage lights slowly come down.*

The End.

A Nick Hern Book

Big Ole Piece of Cake first published in Great Britain as a paperback original in 2010 by Nick Hern Books Limited, 14 Larden Road, London W3 7ST in association with Fishamble: The New Play Company

Big Ole Piece of Cake copyright © 2010 Sean McLoughlin

Sean McLoughlin has asserted his right to be identified as the author of this work

Cover photograph by Patrick Redmond with Ian-Lloyd Anderson as Colin, Joe Hanley as Ray and Mark Lambert as Clarence
Cover design by Ned Hoste, 2H

Typeset by Nick Hern Books, London
Printed and bound by CLE Print Ltd, St Ives, Cambs, PE27 3LE

A CIP catalogue record for this book is available from the British Library

ISBN 978 1 84842 140 0

CAUTION   All rights whatsoever in this play are strictly reserved. Requests to reproduce the text in whole or in part should be addressed to the publisher.

Amateur Performing Rights   Applications for performance, including readings and excerpts, in the English language throughout the world by amateurs (excluding stock companies in the United States of America and Canada) should be addressed to the Performing Rights Manager, Nick Hern Books, 14 Larden Road, London W3 7ST, *tel* +44 (0)20 8749 4953, *fax* +44 (0)20 8735 0250, *e-mail* info@nickhernbooks.demon.co.uk, except as follows:

Australia: Dominie Drama, 8 Cross Street, Brookvale 2100, *fax* (2) 9938 8695, *e-mail* drama@dominie.com.au

New Zealand: Play Bureau, PO Box 420, New Plymouth, *fax* (6)753 2150, *e-mail* play.bureau.nz@xtra.co.nz

South Africa: DALRO (pty) Ltd, PO Box 31627, 2017 Braamfontein, *tel* (11) 712 8000, *fax* (11) 403 9094, *e-mail* theatricals@dalro.co.za

Professional Performing Rights   Applications for performance by professionals in any medium and in any language throughout the world (including by stock companies in the United States of America and Canada) should be addressed to Knight Hall Agency, Lower Ground, 7 Mallow Street, London EC1Y 8RQ, *e-mail* office@knighthallagency.com

No performance of any kind may be given unless a licence has been obtained. Applications should be made before rehearsals begin. Publication of this play does not necessarily indicate its availability for performance.

FSC
The mark of responsible forestry
TT-COC-003115
FSC Trademark © 1996 Forest Stewardship Council A.C